Pygmalion
George
Bernard Shaw

WASHINGTON SQUARE PRESS
PUBLISHED BY POCKET BOOKS

New York   London   Toronto   Sydney   Tokyo

ACKNOWLEDGMENTS

"Pygmalion and Galatea," by Steele Savage. From *Mythology* by Edith Hamilton, illustrated by Steele Savage. Copyright 1940, 1942 by Edith Hamilton. Reprinted by permission of the publishers, Little, Brown and Company, Boston.

Photograph of George Bernard Shaw by Yousuf Karsh. © KARSH from Rapho Guillumette. Reprinted with permission.

"Looking for taxis on a rainy night in London—early 1900's," by C. H. Taffs. From *The Graphic*. Copyright Illustrated Newspapers.

"Bathroom—early 1900's." "Lisbeth" by Carl Larsson. From *"Lässt Licht Hinein"* by Carl Larsson. Reprinted by permission of Albert Bonniers Förlag AB.

Movie stills from *My Fair Lady*. Reprinted with permission of Warner Brothers.

Acknowledgment is made to The Society of Authors on behalf of the Bernard Shaw Estate for permission to reprint *Pygmalion*. Applications for permission to give stock and amateur performances of Bernard Shaw's plays in the United States of America and Canada should be made to The Theatre Guild Inc., 23 West 53rd Street, New York, N.Y. 10019. In all other cases, whether for stage, radio or television, applications should be made to The Society of Authors, 84 Drayton Gardens, London, S.W. 10, England.

A Washington Square Press Publication of
POCKET BOOKS, a division of Simon & Schuster Inc.
1230 Avenue of the Americas, New York, N.Y. 10020

ISBN: 0-671-64352-5

First Pocket Books printing July 1973

14 13 12 11 10 9

WASHINGTON SQUARE PRESS and WSP colophon are registered trademarks of Simon & Schuster Inc.

Printed in the U.S.A.

"... I have created this thing
out of the squashed cabbage
leaves of Covent Garden."

The ancient myth of the artist enamored of
his creation underlies Henry Higgins's metamorphosis of Liza Doolittle from a "draggletailed guttersnipe" to a "duchess" who momen-
tarily upsets his hard-edged reserve. Yet George
Bernard Shaw's retelling of his age-old tale
avoids romanticism in order to stress mankind's
belief that human clay can be molded into
wondrous shapes, regardless of origins or
background.

Each ENRICHED CLASSICS edition includes
a Reader's Supplement containing valuable
information about the author's life and times
as well as criticism of his work. The Supple-
ments are prepared under the supervision of
Harry Shefter, Professor of English at New
York University. The contributing editors for this
edition are Hortense Levisohn, formerly
Principal of William Howard Taft High School,
and Leonard Ashley, Professor of English at
Brooklyn College. Grateful acknowledgment is
made to the Picture Collection Division of the
New York Public Library for providing much
of the illustrative material.

THE MYTHOLOGICAL PYGMALION AND HIS STATUE COME
TO LIFE AS HIS BELOVED GALATEA

A NOTE ABOUT THE TEXT

Readers will notice numerous variations from standard American usage in spelling, punctuation, contractions, etc. To have edited these variations would have destroyed not only the authenticity of the text but an insight into Shaw's lifelong contempt for the restraints of convention, even when they applied in so mildly a controversial area as writing mechanics.

The Editors

Preface to PYGMALION

A Professor of Phonetics

As will be seen later on, *Pygmalion* needs, not a preface, but a sequel, which I have supplied in its due place.

The English have no respect for their language, and will not teach their children to speak it. They cannot spell it because they have nothing to spell it with but an old foreign alphabet of which only the consonants—and not all of them—have any agreed speech value. Consequently no man can teach himself what it should sound like from reading it; and it is impossible for an Englishman to open his mouth without making some other Englishman despise him. Most European languages are now accessible in black and white to foreigners: English and French are not thus accessible even to Englishmen and Frenchmen. The reformer we need most today is an energetic enthusiast: that is why I have made such a one the hero of a popular play.

There have been heroes of that kind crying in the wilderness for many years past. When I became interested in the subject towards the end of the eighteen-seventies, the illustrious Alexander Melville Bell, the inventor of Visible Speech, had emigrated to Canada, where his son invented the telephone; but Alexander J. Ellis was still a London Patriarch, with an impressive head always covered by a velvet skull cap, for which he would apologize to public meetings in a very courtly manner. He and Tito Pagliardini, another phonetic veteran, were men whom it was impossible to dislike. Henry Sweet, then a young man, lacked their sweetness of character: he was about as conciliatory to conventional mortals as Ibsen or Samuel Butler. His great ability as a phonetician (he was, I think, the best of them all at his job) would have entitled him to high official recognition, and perhaps enabled him to popularize his subject, but for his Satanic contempt for all academic dignitaries and persons in general who thought more of Greek than of phonetics. Once, in the days when the Imperial Institute rose in South Kensington, and Joseph Chamberlain was booming the Empire, I induced the editor of a leading monthly review to commission an article from Sweet on the imperial importance of his subject. When it arrived, it contained nothing but a savagely derisive attack on a professor of language and literature whose chair Sweet regarded as proper to a phonetic expert only. The article, being libellous, had to be returned as impossible; and I had to renounce my dream of dragging its author into the limelight. When I met him afterwards, for the first time for many years, I found to my astonishment that he, who had been a quite tolerably presentable young man, had actually managed by sheer scorn to alter his personal appearance until he had become a sort of walking repudiation of Oxford and all its traditions. It must have been largely in his own despite that he was squeezed into something called a Readership of phonetics there. The future of phonetics rests probably with his pupils, who all swore by him; but nothing could bring the man himself into any sort of compliance with the university to which he nevertheless clung by divine right in an intensely Oxonian way. I daresay his papers, if he has left any, include some satires that may be published without too destructive results fifty years hence. He was, I believe, not in the least an ill-natured man: very much the opposite, I should say; but he would not suffer fools gladly; and to him all scholars who were not rabid phoneticians were fools.

Those who knew him will recognize in my third act the allusion to the Current Shorthand in which he used to write postcards. It may be acquired from a four and sixpenny manual published by the Clarendon Press. The postcards which Mrs Higgins describes are such as I have received from Sweet. I would decipher a sound which a cockney would represent by *zerr,* and a Frenchman by *seu,* and then write demanding with some heat what on earth it meant. Sweet, with boundless contempt for my stupidity, would reply that it not only meant but obviously was the word Result, as no other word containing that sound, and capable of making sense with the context, existed in any language spoken on earth. That less expert mortals should require fuller indications was beyond Sweet's patience. Therefore, though the whole point of his Current Shorthand is that it can express every sound in the language perfectly, vowels as well as consonants, and that your hand has to make no stroke except the easy and current ones with which you write m, n, and u, l, p, and q, scribbling them at whatever angle comes easiest to you, his unfortunate determination to make this remarkable and quite legible script serve also as a shorthand reduced it in his own practice to the most inscrutable of cryptograms. His true objective was the provision of a full, accurate, legible script for our language; but he was led past that by his contempt for the popular Pitman system of shorthand, which he called the Pitfall system. The triumph of Pitman was a triumph of business organization: there was a weekly paper to persuade you to learn Pitman; there were cheap textbooks and exercise books and transcripts of speeches for you to copy, and schools where experienced teachers coached you up to the necessary proficiency. Sweet could not organize his market in that fashion. He might as well have been the Sybil who tore up the leaves of prophecy that nobody would attend

to. The four and sixpenny manual, mostly in his litho-
graphed handwriting, that was never vulgarly advertized,
may perhaps some day be taken up by a syndicate and
pushed upon the public as *The Times* pushed the *Ency-
clopædia Britannica*; but until then it will certainly not
prevail against Pitman. I have bought three copies of it
during my lifetime; and I am informed by the publishers
that its cloistered existence is still a steady and healthy
one. I actually learned the system two several times; and
yet the shorthand in which I am writing these lines is
Pitman's. And the reason is, that my secretary cannot
transcribe Sweet, having been perforce taught in the
schools of Pitman. In America I could use the com-
mercially organized Gregg shorthand, which has taken a
hint from Sweet by making its letters writable (current,
Sweet would have called them) instead of having to be
geometrically drawn like Pitman's; but all these systems,
including Sweet's, are spoilt by making them available
for verbatim reporting, in which complete and exact
spelling and word division are impossible. A complete
and exact phonetic script is neither practicable nor
necessary for ordinary use; but if we enlarge our alphabet
to the Russian size, and make our spelling as phonetic as
Spanish, the advance will be prodigious.

Pygmalion Higgins is not a portrait of Sweet, to whom
the adventure of Eliza Doolittle would have been impossible; still, as will be seen, there are touches of Sweet
in the play. With Higgins's physique and temperament
Sweet might have set the Thames on fire. As it was, he
impressed himself professionally on Europe to an extent
that made his comparative personal obscurity, and the
failure of Oxford to do justice to his eminence, a puzzle
to foreign specialists in his subject. I do not blame Oxford, because I think Oxford is quite right in demanding
a certain social amenity from its nurslings (heaven knows

it is not exorbitant in its requirement!); for although I well know how hard it is for a man of genius with a seriously underrated subject to maintain serene and kindly relations with the men who underrate it, and who keep all the best places for less important subjects which they profess without originality and sometimes without much capacity for them, still, if he overwhelms them with wrath and disdain, he cannot expect them to heap honors on him.

Of the later generations of phoneticians I know little. Among them towered Robert Bridges, to whom perhaps Higgins may owe his Miltonic sympathies, though here again I must disclaim all portraiture. But if the play makes the public aware that there are such people as phoneticians, and that they are among the most important people in England at present, it will serve its turn.

I wish to boast that *Pygmalion* has been an extremely successful play, both on stage and screen, all over Europe and North America as well as at home. It is so intensely and deliberately didactic, and its subject is esteemed so dry, that I delight in throwing it at the heads of the wiseacres who repeat the parrot cry that art should never be didactic. It goes to prove my contention that great art can never be anything else.

Finally, and for the encouragement of people troubled with accents that cut them off from all high employment, I may add that the change wrought by Professor Higgins in the flower girl is neither impossible nor uncommon. The modern concierge's daughter who fulfills her ambition by playing the Queen of Spain in *Ruy Blas* at the Théâtre Français is only one of many thousands of men and women who have sloughed off their native dialects and acquired a new tongue. Our West End shop assistants and domestic servants are bilingual. But the thing has to be done scientifically, or the last state of the aspirant may be worse than the first. An honest slum dialect is more tolerable than the attempts of phonetically untaught persons to imitate the plutocracy. Ambitious flower girls who read this play must not imagine that they can pass themselves off as fine ladies by untutored imitation. They must learn their alphabet over again, and differently, from a phonetic expert. Imitation will only make them ridiculous.

NOTE FOR TECHNICIANS. A complete representation of the play as printed in this edition is technically possible only on the cinema screen or on stages furnished with exceptionally elaborate machinery. For ordinary theatrical use the scenes separated by rows of asterisks are to be omitted.

In the dialogue an e upside down indicates the indefinite vowel, sometimes called obscure or neutral, for which, though it is one of the commonest sounds in English speech, our wretched alphabet has no letter.

PYGMALION

— • • —

ACT I

PYGMALION

———— • • ————

ACT I

London at 11.15 p.m. Torrents of heavy summer rain. Cab whistles blowing frantically in all directions. Pedestrians running for shelter into the portico of St. Paul's church (not Wren's cathedral but Inigo Jones's church in Covent Garden vegetable market), among them a lady and her daughter in evening dress. All are peering out gloomily at the rain, except one man with his back turned to the rest, wholly preoccupied with a notebook in which he is writing.

The church clock strikes the first quarter.

THE DAUGHTER [in the space between the central pillars, close to the one on her left] I'm getting chilled to the bone. What can Freddy be doing all this time? He's been gone twenty minutes.

THE MOTHER [on her daughter's right] Not so long. But he ought to have got us a cab by this.

A BYSTANDER [on the lady's right] He wont get no cab not until half-past eleven, missus, when they come back after dropping their theatre fares.

THE MOTHER. But we must have a cab. We cant stand here until half-past eleven. It's too bad.

THE BYSTANDER. Well, it aint my fault, missus.

THE DAUGHTER. If Freddy had a bit of gumption, he would have got one at the theatre door.

THE MOTHER. What could he have done, poor boy?

THE DAUGHTER. Other people got cabs. Why couldnt he?

Freddy rushes in out of the rain from the Southampton Street side, and comes between them closing a dripping umbrella. He is a young man of twenty, in evening dress, very wet round the ankles.

THE DAUGHTER. Well, havnt you got a cab?

FREDDY. Theres not one to be had for love or money.

THE MOTHER. Oh, Freddy, there must be one. You cant have tried.

THE DAUGHTER. It's too tiresome. Do you expect us to go and get one ourselves?

FREDDY. I tell you theyre all engaged. The rain was so sudden: nobody was prepared; and everybody had to take a cab. Ive been to Charing Cross one way and nearly to Ludgate Circus the other; and they were all engaged.

THE MOTHER. Did you try Trafalgar Square?

FREDDY. There wasnt one at Trafalgar Square.

THE DAUGHTER. Did you try?

FREDDY. I tried as far as Charing Cross Station. Did you expect me to walk to Hammersmith?

THE DAUGHTER. You havnt tried at all.

THE MOTHER. You really are very helpless, Freddy. Go again; and dont come back until you have found a cab.

FREDDY. I shall simply get soaked for nothing.

THE DAUGHTER. And what about us? Are we to stay here all night in this draught, with next to nothing on? You selfish pig—

FREDDY. Oh, very well: I'll go, I'll go. [*He opens his umbrella and dashes off Strandwards, but comes into collision with a flower girl who is hurrying in for shelter, knocking her basket out of her hands. A blinding flash of lightning, followed instantly by a rattling peal of thunder, orchestrates the incident*].

THE FLOWER GIRL. Nah then, Freddy: look wh' y' gowin, deah.

FREDDY. Sorry [*he rushes off*].

THE FLOWER GIRL [*picking up her scattered flowers and replacing them in the basket*] Theres menners f' yer! Tə-oo banches o voylets trod into the mad. [*She sits down on the plinth of the column, sorting her flowers, on the lady's right. She is not at all a romantic figure. She is perhaps eighteen, perhaps twenty, hardly older. She wears a little sailor hat of black straw that has long been exposed to the dust and soot of London and has seldom if ever been brushed. Her hair needs washing rather badly: its mousy color can hardly be natural. She wears a shoddy black coat that reaches nearly to her knees and is shaped to her waist. She has a brown skirt with a coarse apron. Her boots are much the worse for wear. She is no doubt as clean as she can afford to be; but compared to the ladies she is very dirty. Her features are no worse than theirs; but their condition leaves something to be desired; and she needs the services of a dentist].*

THE MOTHER. How do you know that my son's name is Freddy, pray?

THE FLOWER GIRL. Ow, eez yə-ooa san, is e? Wal, fewd dan y' də-ooty bawmz a mather should, eed now bettern to spawl a pore gel's flahrzn than ran awy athaht pyin. Will ye-oo py me f'them? [*Here, with apologies, this desperate attempt to represent her dialect without a phonetic alphabet must be abandoned as unintelligible outside London*].

THE DAUGHTER. Do nothing of the sort, mother. The idea!

THE MOTHER. Please allow me, Clara. Have you any pennies?

THE DAUGHTER. No. Ive nothing smaller than sixpence.

THE FLOWER GIRL [*hopefully*] I can give you change for a tanner, kind lady.

THE MOTHER [*to Clara*] Give it to me. [*Clara parts reluctantly*]. Now [*to the girl*] This is for your flowers.

THE FLOWER GIRL. Thank you kindly, lady.

THE DAUGHTER. Make her give you the change. These things are only a penny a bunch.

THE MOTHER. Do hold your tongue, Clara. [*To the girl*] You can keep the change.

THE FLOWER GIRL. Oh, thank you, lady.

THE MOTHER. Now tell me how you know that young gentleman's name.

THE FLOWER GIRL. I didnt.

THE MOTHER. I heard you call him by it. Dont try to deceive me.

THE FLOWER GIRL [*protesting*] Who's trying to deceive you? I called him Freddy or Charlie same as you might yourself if you was talking to a stranger and wished to be pleasant.

THE DAUGHTER. Sixpence thrown away! Really, mamma, you might have spared Freddy that. [*She retreats in disgust behind the pillar*].

An elderly gentleman of the amiable military type rushes into the shelter, and closes a dripping umbrella. He is in the same plight as Freddy, very wet about the ankles. He is in evening dress, with a light overcoat. He takes the place left vacant by the daughter.

THE GENTLEMAN. Phew!

THE MOTHER [*to the gentleman*] Oh, sir, is there any sign of its stopping?

THE GENTLEMAN. I'm afraid not. It started worse than ever about two minutes ago [*he goes to the plinth beside the flower girl; puts up his foot on it; and stoops to turn down his trouser ends*].

THE MOTHER. Oh dear! [*She retires sadly and joins her daughter*].

THE FLOWER GIRL [*taking advantage of the military gentleman's proximity to establish friendly relations with him*] If it's worse, it's a sign it's nearly over. So cheer up, Captain; and buy a flower off a poor girl.

THE GENTLEMAN. I'm sorry. I havnt any change.

THE FLOWER GIRL. I can give you change, Captain.

THE GENTLEMAN. For a sovereign? Ive nothing less.

THE FLOWER GIRL. Garn! Oh do buy a flower off me, Captain. I can change half-a-crown. Take this for tuppence.

THE GENTLEMAN. Now dont be troublesome: theres a good girl. [*Trying his pockets*] I really havnt any change—Stop: heres three hapence, if thats any use to you [*he retreats to the other pillar*].

THE FLOWER GIRL [*disappointed, but thinking three half-pence better than nothing*] Thank you, sir.

THE BYSTANDER [*to the girl*] You be careful: give him a flower for it. Theres a bloke here behind taking down every blessed word youre saying. [*All turn to the man who is taking notes*].

THE FLOWER GIRL [*springing up terrified*] I aint done nothing wrong by speaking to the gentleman. Ive a right to sell flowers if I keep off the kerb. [*Hysterically*] I'm a respectable girl: so help me, I never spoke to him except to ask him to buy a flower off me.

General hubbub, mostly sympathetic to the flower girl, but deprecating her excessive sensibility. Cries of Dont start hollerin. Who's hurting you? Nobody's going to touch you. Whats the good of fussing? Steady on. Easy easy, etc., *come from the elderly staid spectators, who pat her comfortingly. Less patient ones bid her shut her head, or ask her roughly what is wrong with her. A remoter group, not knowing what the matter is, crowd in and increase the noise with question and answer:* Whats the row? What-she do? Where is he? A tec taking her down. What! him? Yes: him over there: Took money off the gentleman, etc.

THE FLOWER GIRL [*breaking through them to the gentleman, crying wildly*] Oh, sir, dont let him charge me. You dunno what it means to me. Theyll take away my character and drive me on the streets for speaking to gentlemen. They—

THE NOTE TAKER [*coming forward on her right, the rest crowding after him*] There! there! there! there! who's hurting you, you silly girl? What do you take me for?

THE BYSTANDER. It's aw rawt: e's a genleman: look at his bə-oots. [*Explaining to the note taker*] She thought you was a copper's nark, sir.

THE NOTE TAKER [*with quick interest*] Whats a copper's nark?

THE BYSTANDER [*inapt at definition*] It's a—well, it's a copper's nark, as you might say. What else would you call it? A sort of informer.

THE FLOWER GIRL [*still hysterical*] I take my Bible oath I never said a word—

THE NOTE TAKER [*overbearing but good-humored*] Oh, shut up, shut up. Do I look like a policeman?

THE FLOWER GIRL [*far from reassured*] Then what did you take down my words for? How do I know whether you took me down right? You just shew me what youve wrote about me. [*The note taker opens his book and holds it steadily under her nose, though the pressure of the mob trying to read it over his shoulders would upset a weaker man*]. Whats that? That aint proper writing. I cant read that.

THE NOTE TAKER. I can. [*Reads, reproducing her pronunciation exactly*] "Cheer ap, Keptin; n' baw ya flahr orf a pore gel."

THE FLOWER GIRL [*much distressed*] It's because I called him Captain. I meant no harm. [*To the gentleman*] Oh, sir, dont let him lay a charge agen me for a word like that. You—

THE GENTLEMAN. Charge! I make no charge. [*To the note taker*] Really, sir, if you are a detective, you need not begin protecting me against molestation by young women until I ask you. Anybody could see that the girl meant no harm.

THE BYSTANDERS GENERALLY [*demonstrating against police espionage*] Course they could. What business is it of yours? You mind your own affairs. He wants promotion, he does. Taking down people's words! Girl never said a word to him. What harm if she did? Nice thing a girl cant shelter from the rain without being insulted, etc., etc., etc. [*She is conducted by the more sympathetic demonstrators back to her plinth, where she resumes her seat and struggles with her emotion*].

THE BYSTANDER. He aint a tec. He's a bloming busybody: thats what he is. I tell you, look at his be-oots.

THE NOTE TAKER [*turning on him genially*] And how are all your people down at Selsey?

THE BYSTANDER [*suspiciously*] Who told you my people come from Selsey?

THE NOTE TAKER. Never you mind. They did. [*To the girl*] How do you come to be up so far east? You were born in Lisson Grove.

THE FLOWER GIRL [*appalled*] Oh, what harm is there in my leaving Lisson Grove? It wasnt fit for a pig to live in; and I had to pay four-and-six a week. [*In tears*] Oh, boo—hoo—oo—

THE NOTE TAKER. Live where you like; but stop that noise.

THE GENTLEMAN [*to the girl*] Come, come! he cant touch you: you have a right to live where you please.

A SARCASTIC BYSTANDER [*thrusting himself between the note taker and the gentleman*] Park Lane, for instance. I'd like to go into the Housing Question with you, I would.

THE FLOWER GIRL [*subsiding into a brooding melancholy over her basket, and talking very low-spiritedly to herself*] I'm a good girl, I am.

THE SARCASTIC BYSTANDER [*not attending to her*] Do you know where I còme from?

THE NOTE TAKER [*promptly*] Hoxton.

Titterings. Popular interest in the note taker's performance increases.

THE SARCASTIC ONE [*amazed*] Well, who said I didnt? Bly me! you know everything, you do.

THE FLOWER GIRL [*still nursing her sense of injury*] Aint no call to meddle with me, he aint.

THE BYSTANDER [*to her*] Of course he aint. Dont you stand

it from him. [*To the note taker*] See here: what call have you to know about people what never offered to meddle with you?

THE FLOWER GIRL. Let him say what he likes. I dont want to have no truck with him.

THE BYSTANDER. You take us for dirt under your feet, dont you? Catch you taking liberties with a gentleman!

THE SARCASTIC BYSTANDER. Yes: tell him where he come from if you want to go fortune-telling.

THE NOTE TAKER. Cheltenham, Harrow, Cambridge, and India.

THE GENTLEMAN. Quite right.

Great laughter. Reaction in the note taker's favor. Exclamations of He knows all about it. Told him proper. Hear him tell the toff where he come from? etc.

THE GENTLEMAN. May I ask, sir, do you do this for your living at a music hall?

THE NOTE TAKER. I've thought of that. Perhaps I shall some day.

The rain has stopped; and the persons on the outside of the crowd begin to drop off.

THE FLOWER GIRL [*resenting the reaction*] He's no gentleman, he aint, to interfere with a poor girl.

THE DAUGHTER [*out of patience, pushing her way rudely to the front and displacing the gentleman, who politely retires to the other side of the pillar*] What on earth is Freddy doing? I shall get pneumownia if I stay in this draught any longer.

THE NOTE TAKER [*to himself, hastily making a note of her pronunciation of "monia"*] Earlscourt.

THE DAUGHTER [*violently*] Will you please keep your impertinent remarks to yourself.

THE NOTE TAKER. Did I say that out loud? I didnt mean to. I beg your pardon. Your mother's Epsom, unmistakeably.

THE MOTHER [*advancing between the daughter and the note taker*] How very curious! I was brought up in Largelady Park, near Epsom.

THE NOTE TAKER [*uproariously amused*] Ha! ha! What a devil of a name! Excuse me. [*To the daughter*] You want a cab, do you?

THE DAUGHTER. Don't dare speak to me.

THE MOTHER. Oh please, please, Clara. [*Her daughter repudiates her with an angry shrug and retires haughtily*] We should be so grateful to you, sir, if you found us a cab. [*The note taker produces a whistle*] Oh, thank you. [*She joins her daughter*].

The note taker blows a piercing blast.

THE SARCASTIC BYSTANDER. There! I knowed he was a plain-clothes copper.

THE BYSTANDER. That aint a police whistle: thats a sporting whistle.

THE FLOWER GIRL [*still preoccupied with her wounded feelings*] He's no right to take away my character. My character is the same to me as any lady's.

THE NOTE TAKER. I dont know whether youve noticed it; but the rain stopped about two minutes ago.

THE BYSTANDER. So it has. Why didnt you say so before? and us losing our time listening to your silliness! [*He walks off towards the Strand*].

THE SARCASTIC BYSTANDER. I can tell where you come from. You come from Anwell. Go back there.

THE NOTE TAKER [*helpfully*] Hanwell.

THE SARCASTIC BYSTANDER [*affecting great distinction of speech*] Thenk you, teacher. Haw haw! So long [*he touches his hat with mock respect and strolls off*].

THE FLOWER GIRL. Frightening people like that! How would he like it himself?

THE MOTHER. It's quite fine now, Clara. We can walk to a motor bus. Come. [*She gathers her skirts above her ankles and hurries off towards the Strand*].

THE DAUGHTER. But the cab—[*her mother is out of hearing*]. Oh, how tiresome! [*She follows angrily*].

All the rest have gone except the note taker, the gentleman, and the flower girl, who sits arranging her basket, and still pitying herself in murmurs.

THE FLOWER GIRL. Poor girl! Hard enough for her to live without being worrited and chivied.

THE GENTLEMAN [*returning to his former place on the note taker's left*] How do you do it, if I may ask?

THE NOTE TAKER. Simply phonetics. The science of speech. Thats my profession: also my hobby. Happy is the man who can make a living by his hobby! You can spot an Irishman or a Yorkshireman by his brogue. *I* can place any man within six miles. I can place him within two miles in London. Some-times within two streets.

THE FLOWER GIRL. Ought to be ashamed of himself, unmanly coward!

THE GENTLEMAN. But is there a living in that?

THE NOTE TAKER. Oh yes. Quite a fat one. This is an age of upstarts. Men begin in Kentish Town with £80 a year, and end in Park Lane with a hundred thousand. They want to drop Kentish Town; but they give themselves away every time they open their mouths. Now I can teach them—

THE FLOWER GIRL. Let him mind his own business and leave a poor girl—

THE NOTE TAKER [*explosively*] Woman: cease this detestable boohooing instantly; or else seek the shelter of some other place of worship.

THE FLOWER GIRL [*with feeble defiance*] Ive a right to be here if I like, same as you.

THE NOTE TAKER. A woman who utters such depressing and disgusting sounds has no right to be anywhere—no right to live. Remember that you are a human being with a soul and the divine gift of articulate speech: that your native language is the language of Shakespeare and Milton and The Bible; and dont sit there crooning like a bilious pigeon.

THE FLOWER GIRL [*quite overwhelmed, looking up at him in mingled wonder and deprecation without daring to raise her head*] Ah-ah-ah-ow-ow-ow-oo!

THE NOTE TAKER [*whipping out his book*] Heavens! what a sound! [*He writes; then holds out the book and reads, reproducing her vowels exactly*] Ah-ah-ah-ow-ow-ow-oo!

THE FLOWER GIRL [*tickled by the performance, and laughing in spite of herself*] Garn!

THE NOTE TAKER. You see this creature with her kerbstone English: the English that will keep her in the gutter to the end of her days. Well, sir, in three months I could pass that girl off as a duchess at an ambassador's garden party. I could even get her a place as lady's maid or shop assistant, which requires better English.

THE FLOWER GIRL. Whats that you say?

THE NOTE TAKER. Yes, you squashed cabbage leaf, you disgrace to the noble architecture of these columns, you incarnate insult to the English language: I could pass you off as the Queen of Sheba. [*To the Gentleman*] Can you believe that?

THE GENTLEMAN. Of course I can. I am myself a student of Indian dialects; and—

THE NOTE TAKER [*eagerly*] Are you? Do you know Colonel Pickering, the author of Spoken Sanscrit?

THE GENTLEMAN. I am Colonel Pickering. Who are you?

THE NOTE TAKER. Henry Higgins, author of Higgins's Universal Alphabet.

PICKERING [*with enthusiasm*] I came from India to meet you.

HIGGINS. I was going to India to meet you.

PICKERING. Where do you live?

HIGGINS. 27A Wimpole Street. Come and see me tomorrow.

PICKERING. I'm at the Carlton. Come with me now and lets have a jaw over some supper.

HIGGINS. Right you are.

THE FLOWER GIRL [*to Pickering, as he passes her*] Buy a flower, kind gentleman. I'm short for my lodging.

PICKERING. I really havnt any change. I'm sorry [*he goes away*].

HIGGINS [*shocked at the girl's mendacity*] Liar. You said you could change half-a-crown.

THE FLOWER GIRL [*rising in desperation*] You ought to be stuffed with nails, you ought. [*Flinging the basket at his feet*] Take the whole blooming basket for sixpence.

The church clock strikes the second quarter.

HIGGINS [*hearing in it the voice of God, rebuking him for his Pharisaic want of charity to the poor girl*] A reminder. [*He raises his hat solemnly; then throws a handful of money into the basket and follows Pickering*].

THE FLOWER GIRL [*picking up a half-crown*] Ah-ow-ooh! [*Picking up a couple of florins*] Aaah-ow-ooh! [*Picking up several coins*] Aaaaah-ow-ooh! [*Picking up a half-sovereign*] Aaaaaaaaaaaah-ow-ooh!!!

FREDDY [*springing out of a taxicab*] Got one at last. Hallo! [*To the girl*] Where are the two ladies that were here?

THE FLOWER GIRL. They walked to the bus when the rain stopped.

FREDDY. And left me with a cab on my hands! Damnation!

THE FLOWER GIRL [*with grandeur*] Never mind, young man. I'm going home in a taxi. [*She sails off to the cab. The driver puts his hand behind him and holds the door firmly shut against her. Quite understanding his mistrust, she shews him her handful of money*]. A taxi fare aint no object to me, Charlie. [*He grins and opens the door*]. Here. What about the basket?

THE TAXIMAN. Give it here. Tuppence extra.

LIZA. No: I dont want nobody to see it. [*She crushes it into the cab and gets in continuing the conversation through the window*] Goodbye, Freddy.

FREDDY [*dazedly raising his hat*] Goodbye.

TAXIMAN. Where to?

LIZA. Bucknam Pellis [Buckingham Palace].

TAXIMAN. What d'ye mean—Bucknam Pellis?

LIZA. Dont you know where it is? In the Green Park, where the King lives. Goodbye, Freddy. Dont let me keep you standing there. Goodbye.

FREDDY. Goodbye. [*He goes*].

TAXIMAN. Here? Whats this about Bucknam Pellis? What business have you at Bucknam Pellis?

LIZA. Of course I havnt none. But I wasnt going to let him know that. You drive me home.

TAXIMAN. And wheres home?

LIZA. Angel Court, Drury Lane, next Meiklejohn's oil shop.

TAXIMAN. That sounds more like it, Judy. [*He drives off*].

❀   ❀   ❀   ❀   ❀   ❀

Let us follow the taxi to the entrance to Angel Court, a narrow little archway between two shops, one of them Meiklejohn's oil shop. When it stops there, Eliza gets out, dragging her basket with her.

LIZA. How much?

TAXIMAN [*indicating the taximeter*] Cant you read? A shilling.

LIZA. A shilling for two minutes!!

TAXIMAN. Two minutes or ten: it's all the same.

LIZA. Well, I dont call it right.

TAXIMAN. Ever been in a taxi before?

LIZA [*with dignity*] Hundreds and thousands of times, young man.

TAXIMAN [*laughing at her*] Good for you, Judy. Keep the shilling, darling, with best love from all at home. Good luck! [*He drives off*].

LIZA [*humiliated*] Impidence!

She picks up the basket and trudges up the alley with it

*to her lodging: a small room with very old wall paper hanging
loose in the damp places. A broken pane in the window is
mended with paper. A portrait of a popular actor and a fashion plate of ladies' dresses, all wildly beyond poor Eliza's
means, both torn from newspapers, are pinned up on the
wall. A birdcage hangs in the window; but its tenant died
long ago: it remains as a memorial only.*

*These are the only visible luxuries: the rest is the irreducible
minimum of poverty's needs: a wretched bed heaped with all
sorts of coverings that have any warmth in them, a draped
packing case with a basin and jug on it and a little looking
glass over it, a chair and table, the refuse of some suburban
kitchen, and an American alarum clock on the shelf above
the unused fireplace: the whole lighted with a gas lamp with
a penny in the slot meter. Rent: four shillings a week.*

Here Eliza, chronically weary, but too excited to go to
bed, sits, counting her new riches and dreaming and planning
what to do with them, until the gas goes out, when she enjoys
for the first time the sensation of being able to put in another
penny without grudging it. This prodigal mood does not
extinguish her gnawing sense of the need for economy sufficiently to prevent her from calculating that she can dream
and plan in bed more cheaply and warmly than sitting up
without a fire. So she takes off her shawl and skirt and adds
them to the miscellaneous bedclothes. Then she kicks off her
shoes and gets into bed without any further change.

PYGMALION

— • • —

ACT II

ACT II

Next day at 11 a.m. Higgins's laboratory in Wimpole Street. It is a room on the first floor, looking on the street, and was meant for the drawing room. The double doors are in the middle of the back wall; and persons entering find in the corner to their right two tall file cabinets at right angles to one another against the walls. In this corner stands a flat writing-table, on which are a phonograph, a laryngoscope, a row of tiny organ pipes with a bellows, a set of lamp chimneys for singing flames with burners attached to a gas plug in the wall by an indiarubber tube, several tuning-forks of different sizes, a life-size image of half a human head, shewing in section the vocal organs, and a box containing a supply of wax cylinders for the phonograph.

Further down the room, on the same side, is a fireplace, with a comfortable leather-covered easy-chair at the side of the hearth nearest the door, and a coal-scuttle. There is a clock on the mantelpiece. Between the fireplace and the phonograph table is a stand for newspapers.

On the other side of the central door, to the left of the visitor, is a cabinet of shallow drawers. On it is a telephone and the telephone directory. The corner beyond, and most of the side wall, is occupied by a grand piano, with the keyboard at the end furthest from the door, and a bench for the players extending the full length of the keyboard. On the piano is a dessert dish heaped with fruit and sweets, mostly chocolates. The middle of the room is clear. Besides the easy-chair, the

*piano bench, and two chairs at the phonograph table, there is
one stray chair. It stands near the fireplace. On the walls, en-
gravings: mostly Piranesis and mezzotint portraits. No paint-
ings.*

*Pickering is seated at the table, putting down some cards
and a tuning-fork which he has been using. Higgins is standing up near him, closing two or three file drawers which are
hanging out. He appears in the morning light as a robust,
vital, appetizing sort of man of forty or thereabouts, dressed
in a professional-looking black frock-coat with a white linen
collar and black silk tie. He is of energetic, scientific type,
heartily, even violently interested in everything that can be
studied as a scientific subject, and careless about himself
and other people, including their feelings. He is, in fact, but
for his years and size, rather like a very impetuous baby
"taking notice" eagerly and loudly, and requiring almost as
much watching to keep him out of unintended mischief. His
manner varies from genial bullying when he is in a good
humor to stormy petulance when anything goes wrong; but
he is so entirely frank and void of malice that he remains
likeable even in his least reasonable moments.*

HIGGINS [*as he shuts the last drawer*] Well, I think thats
the whole show.

PICKERING. It's really amazing. I havnt taken half of it in,
you know.

HIGGINS. Would you like to go over any of it again?

PICKERING [*rising and coming to the fireplace, where he
plants himself with his back to the fire*] No, thank you: not
now. I'm quite done up for this morning.

HIGGINS [*following him, and standing beside him on his
left*] Tired of listening to sounds?

PICKERING. Yes. It's a fearful strain. I rather fancied myself
because I can pronounce twenty-four distinct vowel sounds;
but your hundred and thirty beat me. I cant hear a bit of
difference between most of them.

HIGGINS [*chuckling, and going over to the piano to eat
sweets*] Oh, that comes with practice. You hear no difference
at first; but you keep on listening, and presently you find
theyre all as different as A from B. [*Mrs Pearce looks in: she
is Higgins's housekeeper*]. Whats the matter?

MRS PEARCE [*hesitating, evidently perplexed*] A young
woman asks to see you, sir.

HIGGINS. A young woman! What does she want?

MRS PEARCE. Well, sir, she says youll be glad to see her when you know what she's come about. She's quite a common girl, sir. Very common indeed. I should have sent her away, only I thought perhaps you wanted her to talk into your machines. I hope Ive not done wrong; but really you see such queer people sometimes—youll excuse me, I'm sure, sir—

HIGGINS. Oh, thats all right, Mrs Pearce. Has she an interesting accent?

MRS PEARCE. Oh, something dreadful, sir, really. I dont know how you can take an interest in it.

HIGGINS [to Pickering] Lets have her up. Shew her up, Mrs Pearce [he rushes across to his working table and picks out a cylinder to use on the phonograph].

MRS PEARCE [only half resigned to it] Very well, sir. It's for you to say. [She goes downstairs].

HIGGINS. This is rather a bit of luck. I'll shew you how I make records. We'll set her talking; and I'll take it down first in Bell's Visible Speech; then in broad Romic; and then we'll get her on the phonograph so that you can turn her on as often as you like with the written transcript before you.

MRS PEARCE [returning] This is the young woman, sir.

The flower girl enters in state. She has a hat with three ostrich feathers, orange, sky-blue, and red. She has a nearly clean apron, and the shoddy coat has been tidied a little. The pathos of this deplorable figure, with its innocent vanity and consequential air, touches Pickering, who has already straightened himself in the presence of Mrs Pearce. But as to Higgins, the only distinction he makes between men and women is that when he is neither bullying nor exclaiming to the heavens against some feather-weight cross, he coaxes women as a child coaxes its nurse when it wants to get anything out of her.

HIGGINS [brusquely, recognizing her with unconcealed disappointment, and at once, babylike, making an intolerable grievance of it] Why, this is the girl I jotted down last night. She's no use: Ive got all the records I want of the Lisson Grove lingo; and I'm not going to waste another cylinder on it. [To the girl] Be off with you: I dont want you.

THE FLOWER GIRL. Dont you be so saucy. You aint heard what I come for yet. [To Mrs Pearce, who is waiting at the *door for further instructions*] Did you tell him I come in a taxi?

MRS PEARCE. Nonsense, girl! what do you think a gentleman like Mr Higgins cares what you came in?

THE FLOWER GIRL. Oh, we are proud! He aint above giving lessons, not him: I heard him say so. Well, I aint come here to ask for any compliment; and if my money's not good enough I can go elsewhere.

HIGGINS. Good enough for what?

THE FLOWER GIRL. Good enough for yə-oo. Now you know, dont you? Ive come to have lessons, I am. And to pay for em tə-oo: make no mistake.

HIGGINS [*stupent*] Well!!! [*Recovering his breath with a gasp*] What do you expect me to say to you?

THE FLOWER GIRL. Well, if you was a gentleman, you might ask me to sit down, I think. Dont I tell you I'm bringing you business?

HIGGINS. Pickering: shall we ask this baggage to sit down, or shall we throw her out of the window?

THE FLOWER GIRL [*running away in terror to the piano, where she turns at bay*] Ah-ah-oh-ow-ow-ow-oo! [*Wounded and whimpering*] I wont be called a baggage when Ive offered to pay like any lady.

Motionless, the two men stare at her from the other side of the room, amazed.

PICKERING [*gently*] But what is it you want?

THE FLOWER GIRL. I want to be a lady in a flower shop stead of sellin at the corner of Tottenham Court Road. But they wont take me unless I can talk more genteel. He said he could teach me. Well, here I am ready to pay him—not asking any favor—and he treats me zif I was dirt.

MRS PEARCE. How can you be such a foolish ignorant girl as to think you could afford to pay Mr Higgins?

THE FLOWER GIRL. Why shouldnt I? I know what lessons cost as well as you do; and I'm ready to pay.

HIGGINS. How much?

THE FLOWER GIRL [*coming back to him, triumphant*] Now youre talking! I thought youd come off it when you saw a chance of getting back a bit of what you chucked at me last night. [*Confidentially*] Youd had a drop in, hadnt you?

HIGGINS [*peremptorily*] Sit down.

THE FLOWER GIRL. Oh, if youre going to make a compliment of it——

HIGGINS [*thundering at her*] Sit down.

MRS PEARCE [*severely*] Sit down, girl. Do as youre told.

THE FLOWER GIRL. Ah-ah-ah-ow-ow-oo! [*She stands, half rebellious, half bewildered*].

PICKERING [*very courteous*] Wont you sit down? [*He places the stray chair near the hearthrug between himself and Higgins.*]

LIZA [*coyly*] Dont mind if I do. [*She sits down. Pickering returns to the hearthrug*].

HIGGINS. Whats your name?

THE FLOWER GIRL. Liza Doolittle.

HIGGINS [*declaiming gravely*]

> Eliza, Elizabeth, Betsy and Bess,
> They went to the woods to get a bird's nes':

PICKERING. They found a nest with four eggs in it:

HIGGINS. They took one apiece, and left three in it.

They laugh heartily at their own fun.

LIZA. Oh, dont be silly.

MRS PEARCE [*placing herself behind Eliza's chair*] You mustnt speak to the gentleman like that.

LIZA. Well, why wont he speak sensible to me?

HIGGINS. Come back to business. How much do you propose to pay me for the lessons?

LIZA. Oh, I know whats right. A lady friend of mine gets French lessons for eighteenpence an hour from a real French gentleman. Well, you wouldnt have the face to ask me the same for teaching me my own language as you would for French; so I wont give more than a shilling. Take it or leave it.

HIGGINS [*walking up and down the room, rattling his keys and his cash in his pockets*] You know, Pickering, if you consider a shilling, not as a simple shilling, but as a percentage of this girl's income, it works out as fully equivalent to sixty or seventy guineas from a millionaire.

PICKERING. How so?

HIGGINS. Figure it out. A millionaire has about £150 a day. She earns about half-a-crown.

LIZA [*haughtily*] Who told you I only——

HIGGINS [*continuing*] She offers me two-fifths of her day's income for a lesson. Two-fifths of a millionaire's income for a day would be somewhere about £60. It's handsome. By George, it's enormous! it's the biggest offer I ever had.

LIZA [*rising, terrified*] Sixty pounds! What are you talking about? I never offered you sixty pounds. Where would I get—

HIGGINS. Hold your tongue.

LIZA [*weeping*] But I aint got sixty pounds. Oh—

MRS PEARCE. Dont cry, you silly girl. Sit down. Nobody is going to touch your money.

HIGGINS. Somebody is going to touch you, with a broomstick, if you dont stop snivelling. Sit down.

LIZA [*obeying slowly*] Ah-ah-ah-ow-oo-o! One would think you was my father.

HIGGINS. If I decide to teach you, I'll be worse than two fathers to you. Here [*he offers her his silk handkerchief*]!

LIZA. Whats this for?

HIGGINS. To wipe your eyes. To wipe any part of your face that feels moist. Remember: thats your handkerchief; and thats your sleeve. Dont mistake the one for the other if you wish to become a lady in a shop.

Liza, utterly bewildered, stares helplessly at him.

MRS PEARCE. It's no use talking to her like that, Mr Higgins: she doesnt understand you. Besides, youre quite wrong: she doesnt do it that way at all [*she takes the handkerchief*].

LIZA [*snatching it*] Here! You give me that handkerchief. He gev it to me, not to you.

PICKERING [*laughing*] He did. I think it must be regarded as her property, Mrs Pearce.

MRS PEARCE [*resigning herself*] Serve you right, Mr Higgins.

PICKERING. Higgins: I'm interested. What about the ambassador's garden party? I'll say youre the greatest teacher alive if you make that good. I'll bet you all the expenses of the experiment you cant do it. And I'll pay for the lessons.

LIZA. Oh, you are real good. Thank you, Captain.

HIGGINS [*tempted, looking at her*] It's almost irresistible. She's so deliciously low—so horribly dirty—

LIZA [*protesting extremely*] Ah-ah-ah-ah-ow-ow-oo-oo!!! I aint dirty: I washed my face and hands afore I come, I did.

PICKERING. Youre certainly not going to turn her head with flattery, Higgins.

MRS PEARCE [*uneasy*] Oh, dont say that, sir: theres more ways than one of turning a girl's head; and nobody can do it better than Mr Higgins, though he may not always mean it. I do hope, sir, you wont encourage him to do anything foolish.

HIGGINS [*becoming excited as the idea grows on him*] What is life but a series of inspired follies? The difficulty is to find them to do. Never lose a chance: it doesnt come every day. I shall make a duchess of this draggletailed guttersnipe.

LIZA [*strongly deprecating this view of her*] Ah-ah-ah-ow-ow-oo!

HIGGINS [*carried away*] Yes: in six months—in three if she has a good ear and a quick tongue—I'll take her anywhere and pass her off as anything. We'll start today: now! this moment! Take her away and clean her, Mrs Pearce. Monkey Brand, if it wont come off any other way. Is there a good fire in the kitchen?

MRS PEARCE [*protesting*] Yes; but—

HIGGINS [*storming on*] Take all her clothes off and burn them. Ring up Whitely or somebody for new ones. Wrap her up in brown paper til they come.

LIZA. Youre no gentleman, youre not, to talk of such things. I'm a good girl, I am; and I know what the like of you are, I do.

HIGGINS. We want none of your Lisson Grove prudery here, young woman. Youve got to learn to behave like a duchess. Take her away, Mrs Pearce. If she gives you any trouble, wallop her.

LIZA [*springing up and running between Pickering and Mrs Pearce for protection*] No! I'll call the police, I will.

MRS PEARCE. But Ive no place to put her.

HIGGINS. Put her in the dustbin.

LIZA. Ah-ah-ah-ow-ow-oo!

PICKERING. Oh come, Higgins! be reasonable.

MRS PEARCE [*resolutely*] You must be reasonable, Mr Higgins: really you must. You cant walk over everybody like this.

Higgins, thus scolded, subsides. The hurricane is succeeded by a zephyr of amiable surprise.

HIGGINS [*with professional exquisiteness of modulation*] I walk over everybody! My dear Mrs Pearce, my dear Pickering, I never had the slightest intention of walking over anyone. All I propose is that we should be kind to this poor girl. We must help her to prepare and fit herself for her new station in life. If I did not express myself clearly it was because I did not wish to hurt her delicacy, or yours.

Liza, reassured, steals back to her chair.

MRS PEARCE [*to Pickering*] Well, did you ever hear anything like that, sir?

PICKERING [*laughing heartily*] Never, Mrs Pearce: never.

HIGGINS [*patiently*] Whats the matter?

MRS PEARCE. Well, the matter is, sir, that you cant take a girl up like that as if you were picking up a pebble on the beach.

HIGGINS. Why not?

MRS PEARCE. Why not! But you dont know anything about her. What about her parents? She may be married.

LIZA. Garn!

HIGGINS. There! As the girl very properly says, Garn! Married indeed! Dont you know that a woman of that class looks a worn out drudge of fifty a year after she's married?

LIZA. Whood marry me?

HIGGINS [*suddenly resorting to the most thrillingly beautiful low tones in his best elocutionary style*] By George, Eliza, the streets will be strewn with the bodies of men shooting themselves for your sake before Ive done with you.

MRS PEARCE. Nonsense, sir. You mustnt talk like that to her.

LIZA [*rising and squaring herself determinedly*] I'm going away. He's off his chump, he is. I dont want no balmies teaching me.

HIGGINS [*wounded in his tenderest point by her insensibility to his elocution*] Oh, indeed! I'm mad, am I? Very well, Mrs Pearce: you neednt order the new clothes for her. Throw her out.

LIZA [*whimpering*] Nah-ow. You got no right to touch me.

MRS PEARCE. You see now what comes of being saucy. [*Indicating the door*] This way, please.

LIZA [*almost in tears*] I didnt want no clothes. I wouldnt have taken them [*she throws away the handkerchief*]. I can buy my own clothes.

HIGGINS [*deftly retrieving the handkerchief and intercepting her on her reluctant way to the door*] Youre an ungrateful wicked girl. This is my return for offering to take you out of the gutter and dress you beautifully and make a lady of you.

MRS PEARCE. Stop, Mr Higgins. I wont allow it. It's you that are wicked. Go home to your parents, girl; and tell them to take better care of you.

LIZA. I aint got no parents. They told me I was big enough to earn my own living and turned me out.

MRS PEARCE. Wheres your mother?

LIZA. I aint got no mother. Her that turned me out was my sixth stepmother. But I done without them. And I'm a good girl, I am.

HIGGINS. Very well, then, what on earth is all this fuss about? The girl doesnt belong to anybody—is no use to anybody but me. [*He goes to Mrs Pearce and begins coaxing*]. You can adopt her, Mrs Pearce: I'm sure a daughter would be a great amusement to you. Now dont make any more fuss. Take her downstairs; and—

MRS PEARCE. But whats to become of her? Is she to be paid anything? Do be sensible, sir.

HIGGINS. Oh, pay her whatever is necessary: put it down in the housekeeping book. [*Impatiently*] What on earth will she want with money? She'll have her food and her clothes. She'll only drink if you give her money.

LIZA [*turning on him*] Oh you are a brute. It's a lie: nobody ever saw the sign of liquor on me. [*To Pickering*] Oh, sir: youre a gentleman: dont let him speak to me like that.

PICKERING [*in good-humored remonstrance*] Does it occur to you, Higgins, that the girl has some feelings?

HIGGINS [*looking critically at her*] Oh no, I dont think so. Not any feelings that we need bother about. [*Cheerily*] Have you, Eliza?

LIZA. I got my feelings same as anyone else.

HIGGINS [*to Pickering, reflectively*] You see the difficulty?

PICKERING. Eh? What difficulty?

HIGGINS. To get her to talk grammar. The mere pronunciation is easy enough.

LIZA. I dont want to talk grammar. I want to talk like a lady in a flower-shop.

MRS PEARCE. Will you please keep to the point, Mr Higgins. I want to know on what terms the girl is to be here. Is she to have any wages? And what is to become of her when youve finished your teaching? You must look ahead a little.

HIGGINS [*impatiently*] Whats to become of her if I leave her in the gutter? Tell me that, Mrs Pearce.

MRS PEARCE. Thats her own business, not yours, Mr Higgins.

HIGGINS. Well, when Ive done with her, we can throw her back into the gutter; and then it will be her own business again; so thats all right.

LIZA. Oh, youve no feeling heart in you: you dont care for nothing but yourself. [*She rises and takes the floor resolutely*]. Here! Ive had enough of this. I'm going [*making for the door*]. You ought to be ashamed of yourself, you ought.

HIGGINS [*snatching a chocolate cream from the piano, his eyes suddenly beginning to twinkle with mischief*] Have some chocolates, Eliza.

LIZA [*halting, tempted*] How do I know what might be in them? Ive heard of girls being drugged by the like of you.

Higgins whips out his penknife; cuts a chocolate in two; puts one half into his mouth and bolts it; and offers her the other half.

HIGGINS. Pledge of good faith, Eliza. I eat one half: you eat the other. [*Liza opens her mouth to retort: he pops the half chocolate into it*]. You shall have boxes of them, barrels of them, every day. You shall live on them. Eh?

LIZA [*who has disposed of the chocolate after being nearly choked by it*] I wouldnt have ate it, only I'm too ladylike to take it out of my mouth.

HIGGINS. Listen, Eliza. I think you said you came in a taxi.

LIZA. Well, what if I did? Ive as good a right to take a taxi as anyone else.

HIGGINS. You have, Eliza; and in future you shall have as many taxis as you want. You shall go up and down and round the town in a taxi every day. Think of that, Eliza.

MRS PEARCE. Mr Higgins: youre tempting the girl. It's not right. She should think of the future.

HIGGINS. At her age! Nonsense! Time enough to think of the future when you havnt any future to think of. No, Eliza: do as this lady does: think of other people's futures; but never think of your own. Think of chocolates, and taxis, and gold, and diamonds.

LIZA. No: I dont want no gold and no diamonds. I'm a good girl, I am. [*She sits down again, with an attempt at dignity*].

HIGGINS. You shall remain so, Eliza, under the care of Mrs Pearce. And you shall marry an officer in the Guards, with a beautiful moustache: the son of a marquis, who will disinherit him for marrying you, but will relent when he sees your beauty and goodness—

PICKERING. Excuse me, Higgins; but I really must interfere. Mrs Pearce is quite right. If this girl is to put herself in your hands for six months for an experiment in teaching, she must understand thoroughly what she's doing.

HIGGINS. How can she? She's incapable of understand anything. Besides, do any of us understand what we are doing? If we did, would we ever do it?

PICKERING. Very clever, Higgins; but not to the present point. [*To Eliza*] Miss Doolittle—

LIZA [*overwhelmed*] Ah-ah-ow-oo!

HIGGINS. There! Thats all youll get out of Eliza. Ah-ah-ow-oo! No use explaining. As a military man you ought to know that. Give her her orders: thats enough for her. Eliza: you are to live here for the next six months, learning how to speak beautifully, like a lady in a florist's shop. If youre good and do whatever youre told, you shall sleep in a proper bedroom, and have lots to eat, and money to buy chocolates and take rides in taxis. If youre naughty and idle you will sleep in the back kitchen among the black beetles, and be walloped by Mrs Pearce with a broomstick. At the end of six months you shall go to Buckingham Palace in a carriage, beautifully dressed. If the King finds out youre not a lady, you will be taken by the police to the Tower of London, where your head will be cut off as a warning to other presumptuous flower girls. If you are not found out, you shall have a present of seven-and-sixpence to start life with as a lady in a shop. If you refuse this offer you will be a most ungrateful wicked girl; and the angels will weep for you. [*To Pickering*] Now are you satisfied, Pickering? [*To Mrs Pearce*] Can I put it more plainly and fairly, Mrs Pearce?

MRS PEARCE [*patiently*] I think youd better let me speak to the girl properly in private. I dont know that I can take charge of her or consent to the arrangement at all. Of course I know you dont mean her any harm; but when you get what you call interested in people's accents, you never think or care what may happen to them or you. Come with me, Eliza.

HIGGINS. Thats all right. Thank you, Mrs Pearce. Bundle her off to the bath-room.

LIZA [*rising reluctantly and suspiciously*] Youre a great bully, you are. I wont stay here if I dont like. I wont let nobody wallop me. I never asked to go to Bucknam Palace, I didnt. I was never in trouble with the police, not me. I'm a good girl—

MRS PEARCE. Dont answer back, girl. You dont understand the gentleman. Come with me. [*She leads the way to the door, and holds it open for Eliza*].

LIZA [*as she goes out*] Well, what I say is right. I wont go near the King, not if I'm going to have my head cut off. If I'd known what I was letting myself in for, I wouldnt have come here. I always been a good girl; and I never offered to say a word to him; and I dont owe him nothing; and I dont care; and I wont be put upon; and I have my feelings the same as anyone else—

Mrs Pearce shuts the door; and Eliza's plaints are no longer audible.

*   *   *   *   *   *

Eliza is taken upstairs to the third floor greatly to her surprise; for she expected to be taken down to the scullery. There Mrs Pearce opens a door and takes her into a spare bedroom.

MRS PEARCE. I will have to put you here. This will be your bedroom.

LIZA. O-h, I couldnt sleep here, missus. It's too good for the likes of me. I should be afraid to touch anything. I aint a duchess yet, you know.

MRS PEARCE. You have got to make yourself as clean as the room: then you wont be afraid of it. And you must call me Mrs Pearce, not missus. [*She throws open the door of the dressingroom, now modernized as a bathroom*].

LIZA. Gawd! whats this? Is this where you wash clothes? Funny sort of copper I call it.

MRS PEARCE. It is not a copper. This is where we wash ourselves, Eliza, and where I am going to wash you.

LIZA. You expect me to get into that and wet myself all over! Not me. I should catch my death. I knew a woman did it every Saturday night; and she died of it.

MRS PEARCE. Mr Higgins has the gentleman's bathroom downstairs; and he has a bath every morning, in cold water.

LIZA. Ugh! He's made of iron, that man.

MRS PEARCE. If you are to sit with him and the Colonel and be taught you will have to do the same. They wont like the smell of you if you dont. But you can have the water as hot as you like. There are two taps: hot and cold.

LIZA [*weeping*] I couldnt. I dursnt. It's not natural: it would kill me. Ive never had a bath in my life: not what youd call a proper one.

MRS PEARCE. Well, dont you want to be clean and sweet and decent, like a lady? You know you cant be a nice girl inside if youre a dirty slut outside.

LIZA. Boohoo!!!!

MRS PEARCE. Now stop crying and go back into your room and take off all your clothes. Then wrap yourself in this [*Taking down a gown from its peg and handing it to her*] and come back to me. I will get the bath ready.

LIZA [*all tears*] I cant. I wont. I'm not used to it. Ive never took off all my clothes before. It's not right: it's not decent.

MRS PEARCE. Nonsense, child. Dont you take off all your clothes every night when you go to bed?

LIZA [*amazed*] No. Why should I? I should catch my death. Of course I take off my skirt.

MRS PEARCE. Do you mean that you sleep in the under-clothes you wear in the daytime?

LIZA. What else have I to sleep in?

MRS PEARCE. You will never do that again as long as you live here. I will get you a proper nightdress.

LIZA. Do you mean change into cold things and lie awake shivering half the night? You want to kill me, you do.

MRS PEARCE. I want to change you from a frowzy slut to a clean respectable girl fit to sit with the gentlemen in the study. Are you going to trust me and do what I tell you or be thrown out and sent back to your flower basket?

LIZA. But you dont know what the cold is to me. You dont know how I dread it.

MRS PEARCE. Your bed wont be cold here: I will put a hot water bottle in it. [*Pushing her into the bedroom*] Off with you and undress.

LIZA. Oh, if only I'd known what a dreadful thing it is to be clean I'd never have come. I didnt know when I was well off. I—[*Mrs Pearce pushes her through the door, but leaves it partly open lest her prisoner should take to flight*].

Mrs Pearce puts on a pair of white rubber sleeves, and fills the bath, mixing hot and cold, and testing the result with the bath thermometer. She perfumes it with a handful of bath

*salts and adds a palmful of mustard. She then takes a for-
midable looking long handled scrubbing brush and soaps it
profusely with a ball of scented soap.*

*Eliza comes back with nothing on but the bath gown
huddled tightly round her, a piteous spectacle of abject terror.*

MRS PEARCE. Now come along. Take that thing off.

LIZA. Oh I couldnt, Mrs Pearce: I reely couldnt. I never
done such a thing.

MRS PEARCE. Nonsense. Here: step in and tell me whether
it's hot enough for you.

LIZA. Ah-oo! Ah-oo! It's too hot.

MRS PEARCE [*deftly snatching the gown away and throwing
Eliza down on her back*] It wont hurt you. [*She sets to work
with the scrubbing brush*].

Eliza's screams are heartrending.

     ❋   ❋   ❋   ❋   ❋   ❋

Meanwhile the Colonel has been having it out with Higgins
about Eliza. Pickering has come from the hearth to the chair
and seated himself astride of it with his arms on the back to
cross-examine him.

PICKERING. Excuse the straight question, Higgins. Are you
a man of good character where women are concerned?

HIGGINS [*moodily*] Have you ever met a man of good character where women are concerned?

PICKERING. Yes: very frequently.

HIGGINS [*dogmatically, lifting himself on his hands to the
level of the piano, and sitting on it with a bounce*] Well, I
havnt. I find that the moment I let a woman make friends
with me, she becomes jealous, exacting, suspicious, and a
damned nuisance. I find that the moment I let myself make
friends with a woman, I become selfish and tyrannical.
Women upset everything. When you let them into your life,
you find that the woman is driving at one thing and youre
driving at another.

PICKERING. At what, for example?

HIGGINS [*coming off the piano restlessly*] Oh, Lord knows!
I suppose the woman wants to live her own life; and the man
wants to live his; and each tries to drag the other on to the
wrong track. One wants to go north and the other south;
and the result is that both have to go east, though they both
hate the east wind. [*He sits down on the bench at the key-*

board]. So here I am, a confirmed old bachelor, and likely to remain so.

PICKERING [*rising and standing over him gravely*] Come, Higgins! You know what I mean. If I'm to be in this business I shall feel responsible for that girl. I hope it's understood that no advantage is to be taken of her position.

HIGGINS. What! That thing! Sacred, I assure you. [*Rising to explain*] You see, she'll be a pupil; and teaching would be impossible unless pupils were sacred. Ive taught scores of American millionairesses how to speak English: the best looking women in the world. I'm seasoned. They might as well be blocks of wood. *I* might as well be a block of wood. It's—

Mrs Pearce opens the door. She has Eliza's hat in her hand. Pickering retires to the easy-chair at the hearth and sits down.

HIGGINS [*eagerly*] Well, Mrs Pearce: is it all right?

MRS PEARCE [*at the door*] I just wish to trouble you with a word, if I may, Mr Higgins.

HIGGINS. Yes, certainly. Come in. [*She comes forward*]. Dont burn that, Mrs Pearce. I'll keep it as a curiosity. [*He takes the hat.*]

MRS PEARCE. Handle it carefully, sir, please. I had to promise her not to burn it; but I had better put it in the oven for a while.

HIGGINS [*putting it down hastily on the piano*] Oh! thank you. Well, what have you to say to me?

PICKERING. Am I in the way?

MRS PEARCE. Not in the least, sir. Mr Higgins: will you please be very particular what you say before the girl?

HIGGINS [*sternly*] Of course. I'm always particular about what I say. Why do you say this to me?

MRS PEARCE [*unmoved*] No, sir: youre not at all particular when youve mislaid anything or when you get a little impatient. Now it doesnt matter before me: I'm used to it. But you really must not swear before the girl.

HIGGINS [*indignantly*] I swear! [*Most emphatically*] I never swear. I detest the habit. What the devil do you mean?

MRS PEARCE [*stolidly*] Thats what I mean, sir. You swear a great deal too much. I dont mind your damning and blasting, and what the devil and where the devil and who the devil—

HIGGINS. Mrs Pearce: this language from your lips! Really!

MRS PEARCE [*not to be put off*]—but there is a certain word I must ask you not to use. The girl used it herself when she began to enjoy the bath. It begins with the same letter as bath. She knows no better: she learnt it at her mother's knee. But she must not hear it from your lips.

HIGGINS [*loftily*] I cannot charge myself with having ever uttered it, Mrs Pearce. [*She looks at him steadfastly. He adds, hiding an uneasy conscience with a judicial air*] Except perhaps in a moment of extreme and justified excitement.

MRS PEARCE. Only this morning, sir, you applied it to your boots, to the butter, and to the brown bread.

HIGGINS. Oh, that! Mere alliteration, Mrs Pearce, natural to a poet.

MRS PEARCE. Well, sir, whatever you choose to call it, I beg you not to let the girl hear you repeat it.

HIGGINS. Oh, very well, very well. Is that all?

MRS PEARCE. No, sir. We shall have to be very particular with this girl as to personal cleanliness.

HIGGINS. Certainly. Quite right. Most important.

MRS PEARCE. I mean not to be slovenly about her dress or untidy in leaving things about.

HIGGINS [*going to her solemnly*] Just so. I intended to call your attention to that. [*He passes on to Pickering, who is enjoying the conversation immensely*]. It is these little things that matter, Pickering. Take care of the pence and the pounds will take care of themselves is as true of personal habits as of money. [*He comes to anchor on the hearthrug, with the air of a man in an unassailable position*].

MRS PEARCE. Yes, sir. Then might I ask you not to come down to breakfast in your dressing-gown, or at any rate not to use it as a napkin to the extent you do, sir. And if you would be so good as not to eat everything off the same plate, and to remember not to put the porridge saucepan out of your hand on the clean tablecloth, it would be a better example to the girl. You know you nearly choked yourself with a fish-bone in a jam only last week.

HIGGINS [*routed from the hearthrug and drifting back to the piano*] I may do these things sometimes in absence of mind; but surely I dont do them habitually. [*Angrily*] By the way: my dressing-gown smells most damnably of benzine.

MRS PEARCE. No doubt it does, Mr Higgins. But if you will wipe your fingers—

HIGGINS [*yelling*] Oh very well, very well: I'll wipe them in my hair in future.

MRS PEARCE. I hope youre not offended, Mr Higgins.

HIGGINS [*shocked at finding himself thought capable of an unamiable sentiment*] Not at all, not at all. Youre quite right, Mrs Pearce: I shall be particularly careful before the girl. Is that all?

MRS PEARCE. No, sir. Might she use some of those Japanese dresses you brought from abroad? I really cant put her back into her old things.

HIGGINS. Certainly. Anything you like. Is that all?

MRS PEARCE. Thank you, sir. Thats all. [*She goes out*].

HIGGINS. You know, Pickering, that woman has the most extraordinary ideas about me. Here I am, a shy, diffident sort of man. Ive never been able to feel really grown-up and tremendous, like other chaps. And yet she's firmly persuaded that I'm an arbitrary overbearing bossing kind of person. I cant account for it.

Mrs Pearce returns.

MRS PEARCE. If you please, sir, the trouble's beginning already. Theres a dustman downstairs, Alfred Doolittle, wants to see you. He says you have his daughter here.

PICKERING [*rising*] Phew! I say!

HIGGINS [*promptly*] Send the blackguard up.

MRS PEARCE. Oh, very well, sir. [*She goes out*].

PICKERING. He may not be a blackguard, Higgins.

HIGGINS. Nonsense. Of course he's a blackguard.

PICKERING. Whether he is or not, I'm afraid we shall have some trouble with him.

HIGGINS [*confidently*] Oh no: I think not. If theres any trouble he shall have it with me, not I with him. And we are sure to get something interesting out of him.

PICKERING. About the girl?

HIGGINS. No. I mean his dialect.

PICKERING. Oh!

MRS PEARCE [*at the door*] Doolittle, sir. [*She admits Doolittle and retires*].

Alfred is an elderly but vigorous dustman, clad in the costume of his profession, including a hat with a back brim covering his neck and shoulders. He has well marked and rather interesting features, and seems equally free from fear and conscience. He has a remarkably expressive voice, the result of a habit of giving vent to his feelings without reserve.

His present pose is that of wounded honor and stern resolution.

DOOLITTLE [*at the door, uncertain which of the two gentlemen is his man*] Professor Iggins?

HIGGINS. Here. Good morning. Sit down.

DOOLITTLE. Morning, Governor. [*He sits down magisterially*] I come about a very serious matter, Governor.

HIGGINS [*to Pickering*] Brought up in Hounslow. Mother Welsh, I should think. [*Doolittle opens his mouth, amazed. Higgins continues*] What do you want, Doolittle?

DOOLITTLE [*menacingly*] I want my daughter: thats what I want. See?

HIGGINS. Of course you do. Youre her father, arnt you? You dont suppose anyone else wants her, do you? I'm glad to see you have some spark of family feeling left. She's upstairs. Take her away at once.

DOOLITTLE [*rising, fearfully taken aback*] What!

HIGGINS. Take her away. Do you suppose I'm going to keep your daughter for you?

DOOLITTLE [*remonstrating*] Now, now, look here, Governor. Is this reasonable? Is it fairity to take advantage of a man like this? The girl belongs to me. You got her. Where do I come in? [*He sits down again*].

HIGGINS. Your daughter had the audacity to come to my house and ask me to teach her how to speak properly so that she could get a place in a flower-shop. This gentleman and my housekeeper have been here all the time. [*Bullying him*] How dare you come here and attempt to blackmail me? You sent her here on purpose.

DOOLITTLE [*protesting*] No, Governor.

HIGGINS. You must have. How else could you possibly know that she is here?

DOOLITTLE. Dont take a man up like that, Governor.

HIGGINS. The police shall take you up. This is a plant—a plot to extort money by threats. I shall telephone for the police [*he goes resolutely to the telephone and opens the directory*].

DOOLITTLE. Have I asked you for a brass farthing? I leave it to the gentleman here: have I said a word about money?

HIGGINS [*throwing the book aside and marching down on Doolittle with a poser*] What else did you come for?

DOOLITTLE [*sweetly*] Well, what would a man come for? Be human, Governor.

HIGGINS [*disarmed*] Alfred: did you put her up to it?

DOOLITTLE. So help me, Governor, I never did. I take my Bible oath I aint seen the girl these two months past.

HIGGINS. Then how did you know she was here?

DOOLITTLE ["*most musical, most melancholy*"] I'll tell you, Governor, if youll only let me get a word in. I'm willing to tell you. I'm wanting to tell you. I'm waiting to tell you.

HIGGINS. Pickering: this chap has a certain natural gift of rhetoric. Observe the rhythm of his native woodnotes wild. "I'm willing to tell you: I'm wanting to tell you: I'm waiting to tell you." Sentimental rhetoric! thats the Welsh strain in him. It also accounts for his mendacity and dishonesty.

PICKERING. Oh, please, Higgins: I'm west country myself. [*To Doolittle*] How did you know the girl was here if you didnt send her?

DOOLITTLE. It was like this, Governor. The girl took a boy in the taxi to give him a jaunt. Son of her landlady, he is. He hung about on the chance of her giving him another ride home. Well, she sent him back for her luggage when she heard you was willing for her to stop here. I met the boy at the corner of Long Acre and Endell Street.

HIGGINS. Public house. Yes?

DOOLITTLE. The poor man's club, Governor: why shouldnt I?

PICKERING. Do let him tell his story, Higgins.

DOOLITTLE. He told me what was up. And I ask you, what was my feelings and my duty as a father? I says to the boy, "You bring me the luggage," I says—

PICKERING. Why didnt you go for it yourself?

DOOLITTLE. Landlady wouldnt have trusted me with it, Governor. She's that kind of woman: you know. I had to give the boy a penny afore he trusted me with it, the little swine. I brought it to her just to oblige you like, and make myself agreeable. Thats all.

HIGGINS. How much luggage?

DOOLITTLE. Musical instrument, Governor. A few pictures, a trifle of jewelry, and a bird-cage. She said she didnt want no clothes. What was I to think from that, Governor? I ask you as a parent what was I to think?

HIGGINS. So you came to rescue her from worse than death, eh?

DOOLITTLE [*appreciatively: relieved at being so well understood*] Just so, Governor. Thats right.

PICKERING. But why did you bring her luggage if you intended to take her away?

DOOLITTLE. Have I said a word about taking her away? Have I now?

HIGGINS [*determinedly*] Youre going to take her away, double quick. [*He crosses to the hearth and rings the bell*].

DOOLITTLE [*rising*] No, Governor. Dont say that. I'm not the man to stand in my girl's light. Heres a career opening for her, as you might say; and—

Mrs Pearce opens the door and awaits orders.

HIGGINS. Mrs Pearce: this is Eliza's father. He has come to take her away. Give her to him. [*He goes back to the piano, with an air of washing his hands of the whole affair*].

DOOLITTLE. No. This is a misunderstanding. Listen here—

MRS PEARCE. He cant take her away, Mr Higgins: how can he? You told me to burn her clothes.

DOOLITTLE. Thats right. I cant carry the girl through the streets like a blooming monkey, can I? I put it to you.

HIGGINS. You have put it to me that you want your daughter. Take your daughter. If she has no clothes go out and buy her some.

DOOLITTLE [*desperate*] Wheres the clothes she come in? Did I burn them or did your missus here?

MRS PEARCE. I am the housekeeper, if you please. I have sent for some clothes for your girl. When they come you can take her away. You can wait in the kitchen. This way, please.

Doolittle, much troubled, accompanies her to the door; then hesitates; finally turns confidentially to Higgins.

DOOLITTLE. Listen here, Governor. You and me is men of the world, aint we?

HIGGINS. Oh! Men of the world, are we? Youd better go, Mrs Pearce.

MRS PEARCE. I think so, indeed, sir. [*She goes, with dignity*].

PICKERING. The floor is yours, Mr Doolittle.

DOOLITTLE [*to Pickering*] I thank you, Governor. [*To Higgins, who takes refuge on the piano bench, a little overwhelmed by the proximity of his visitor; for Doolittle has a professional flavour of dust about him*]. Well, the truth is, Ive taken a sort of fancy to you, Governor; and if you want the girl, I'm not so set on having her back home again but what I might be open to an arrangement. Regarded in the light of a young woman, she's a fine handsome girl. As a daughter she's not worth her keep; and so I tell you straight. All I ask is my rights as a father; and youre the last man alive to expect me to let her go for nothing; for I can see youre one of the straight sort, Governor. Well, whats a five-pound note to you? and whats Eliza to me? [*He turns to his chair and sits down judicially*].

PICKERING. I think you ought to know, Doolittle, that Mr Higgins's intentions are entirely honorable.

DOOLITTLE. Course they are, Governor. If I thought they wasnt, I'd ask fifty.

HIGGINS [*revolted*] Do you mean to say that you would sell your daughter for £50?

DOOLITTLE. Not in a general way I would; but to oblige a gentleman like you I'd do a good deal, I do assure you.

PICKERING. Have you no morals, man?

DOOLITTLE [*unabashed*] Cant afford them, Governor. Neither could you if you was as poor as me. Not that I mean any harm, you know. But if Liza is going to have a bit out of this, why not me too?

HIGGINS [*troubled*] I dont know what to do, Pickering. There can be no question that as a matter of morals it's a positive crime to give this chap a farthing. And yet I feel a sort of rough justice in his claim.

DOOLITTLE. Thats it, Governor. Thats all I say. A father's heart, as it were.

PICKERING. Well, I know the feeling; but really it seems hardly right—

DOOLITTLE. Dont say that, Governor. Dont look at it that way. What am I, Governors both? I ask you, what am I? I'm one of the undeserving poor: thats what I am. Think of what that means to a man. It means that he's up agen middle class morality all the time. If theres anything going, and I put in for a bit of it, it's always the same story: "Youre undeserving; so you cant have it." But my needs is as great as the most deserving widow's that ever got money out of six different charities in one week for the death of the same husband. I dont need less than a deserving man: I need more.

I dont eat less hearty than him; and I drink a lot more. I want a bit of amusement, cause I'm a thinking man. I want cheerfulness and a song and a band when I feel low. Well, they charge me just the same for everything as they charge the deserving. What is middle class morality? Just an excuse for never giving me anything. Therefore, I ask you, as two gentlemen, not to play that game on me. I'm playing straight with you. I aint pretending to be deserving. I'm undeserving; and I mean to go on being undeserving. I like it; and thats the truth. Will you take advantage of a man's nature to do him out of the price of his own daughter what he's brought up and fed and clothed by the sweat of his brow until she's growed big enough to be interesting to you two gentlemen? Is five pounds unreasonable? I put it to you; and I leave it to you.

HIGGINS [*rising, and going over to Pickering*] Pickering: if we were to take this man in hand for three months, he could choose between a seat in the Cabinet and a popular pulpit in Wales.

PICKERING. What do you say to that, Doolittle?

DOOLITTLE. Not me, Governor, thank you kindly. Ive heard all the preachers and all the prime ministers—for I'm a thinking man and game for politics or religion or social reform same as all the other amusements—and I tell you it's a dog's life any way you look at it. Undeserving poverty is my line. Taking one station in society with another, it's—it's—well, it's the only one that has any ginger in it, to my taste.

HIGGINS. I suppose we must give him a fiver.

PICKERING. He'll make a bad use of it, I'm afraid.

DOOLITTLE. Not me, Governor, so help me I wont. Dont you be afraid that I'll save it and spare it and live idle on it. There wont be a penny of it left by Monday: I'll have to go to work same as if I'd never had it. It wont pauperize me, you bet. Just one good spree for myself and the missus, giving pleasure to ourselves and employment to others, and satisfaction to you to think it's not been throwed away. You couldn't spend it better.

HIGGINS [*taking out his pocket book and coming between Doolittle and the piano*] This is irresistible. Lets give him ten. [*He offers two notes to the dustman*].

DOOLITTLE. No, Governor. She wouldnt have the heart to spend ten; and perhaps I shouldnt neither. Ten pounds is a lot of money: it makes a man feel prudent like; and then goodbye to happiness. You give me what I ask you, Governor: not a penny more, and not a penny less.

PICKERING. Why dont you marry that missus of yours? I rather draw the line at encouraging that sort of immorality.

DOOLITTLE. Tell her so, Governor: tell her so. I'm willing. It's me that suffers by it. Ive no hold on her. I got to be agreeable to her. I got to give her presents. I got to buy her clothes something sinful. I'm a slave to that woman, Governor, just because I'm not her lawful husband. And she knows it too. Catch her marrying me! Take my advice, Governor: marry Eliza while she's young and dont know no better. If you dont youll be sorry for it after. If you do, she'll be sorry for it after; but better her than you, because youre a man, and she's only a woman and dont know how to be happy anyhow.

HIGGINS. Pickering: if we listen to this man another minute, we shall have no convictions left. [*To Doolittle*] Five pounds I think you said.

DOOLITTLE. Thank you kindly, Governor.

HIGGINS. Youre sure you wont take ten?

DOOLITTLE. Not now. Another time, Governor.

HIGGINS [*handing him a five-pound note*] Here you are.

DOOLITTLE. Thank you, Governor. Good morning. [*He hurries to the door, anxious to get away with his booty. When he opens it he is confronted with a dainty and exquisitely clean young Japanese lady in a simple blue cotton kimono printed cunningly with small white jasmine blossoms. Mrs Pearce is with her. He gets out of her way deferentially and apologizes*]. Beg pardon, miss.

THE JAPANESE LADY. Garn! Dont you know your own daughter?

DOOLITTLE	*exclaiming*	Bly me! it's Eliza!
HIGGINS	*simul-*	Whats that? This!
PICKERING	*taneously*	By Jove!

LIZA. Dont I look silly?

HIGGINS. Silly?

MRS PEARCE [*at the door*] Now, Mr Higgins, please dont say anything to make the girl conceited about herself.

HIGGINS [*conscientiously*] Oh! Quite right, Mrs Pearce. [*To Eliza*] Yes: damned silly.

MRS PEARCE. Please, sir.

HIGGINS [*correcting himself*] I mean extremely silly.

LIZA. I should look all right with my hat on. [*She takes up her hat; puts it on; and walks across the room to the fireplace with a fashionable air*].

HIGGINS. A new fashion, by George! And it ought to look horrible!

DOOLITTLE [*with fatherly pride*] Well, I never thought she'd clean up as good looking as that, Governor. She's a credit to me, aint she?

LIZA. I tell you, it's easy to clean up here. Hot and cold water on tap, just as much as you like, there is. Woolly towels, there is; and a towel horse so hot, it burns your fingers. Soft brushes to scrub yourself, and a wooden bowl of soap smelling like primroses. Now I know why ladies is so clean. Washing's a treat for them. Wish they could see what it is for the like of me!

HIGGINS. I'm glad the bathroom met with your approval.

LIZA. It didnt: not all of it; and I dont care who hears me say it. Mrs Pearce knows.

HIGGINS. What was wrong, Mrs Pearce?

MRS PEARCE [*blandly*] Oh, nothing, sir. It doesnt matter.

LIZA. I had a good mind to break it. I didnt know which way to look. But I hung a towel over it, I did.

HIGGINS. Over what?

MRS PEARCE. Over the looking-glass, sir.

HIGGINS. Doolittle: you have brought your daughter up too strictly.

DOOLITTLE. Me! I never brought her up at all, except to give her a lick of a strap now and again. Dont put it on me, Governor. She aint accustomed to it, you see: thats all. But she'll soon pick up your free-and-easy ways.

LIZA. I'm a good girl, I am; and I wont pick up no free-and-easy ways.

HIGGINS. Eliza: if you say again that youre a good girl, your father shall take you home.

LIZA. Not him. You dont know my father. All he come here for was to touch you for some money to get drunk on.

DOOLITTLE. Well, what else would I want money for? To put into the plate in church, I suppose. [*She puts out her tongue at him. He is so incensed by this that Pickering presently finds it necessary to step between them*]. Dont you give me none of your lip; and dont let me hear you giving this gentleman any of it neither, or youll hear from me about it. See?

HIGGINS. Have you any further advice to give her before you go, Doolittle? Your blessing, for instance.

DOOLITTLE. No, Governor: I aint such a mug as to put up my children to all I know myself. Hard enough to hold them in without that. If you want Eliza's mind improved, Governor, you do it yourself with a strap. So long, gentlemen. [He turns to go].

HIGGINS [impressively] Stop. Youll come regularly to see your daughter. It's your duty, you know. My brother is a clergyman; and he could help you in your talks with her.

DOOLITTLE [evasively] Certainly, I'll come, Governor. Not just this week, because I have a job at a distance. But later on you may depend on me. Afternoon, gentlemen. Afternoon, maam. [He touches his hat to Mrs Pearce, who disdains the salutation and goes out. He winks at Higgins, thinking him probably a fellow-sufferer from Mrs Pearce's difficult disposition, and follows her].

LIZA. Dont you believe the old liar. He'd as soon you set a bulldog on him as a clergyman. You wont see him again in a hurry.

HIGGINS. I dont want to, Eliza. Do you?

LIZA. Not me. I dont want never to see him again, I dont. He's a disgrace to me, he is, collecting dust, instead of working at his trade.

PICKERING. What is his trade, Eliza?

LIZA. Talking money out of other people's pockets into his own. His proper trade's a navvy; and he works at it sometimes too—for exercise—and earns good money at it. Aint you going to call me Miss Doolittle any more?

PICKERING. I beg your pardon, Miss Doolittle. It was a slip of the tongue.

LIZA. Oh, I dont mind; only it sounded so genteel. I should just like to take a taxi to the corner of Tottenham Court Road and get out there and tell it to wait for me, just to put the girls in their place a bit. I wouldnt speak to them, you know.

PICKERING. Better wait til we get you something really fashionable.

HIGGINS. Besides, you shouldnt cut your old friends now that you have risen in the world. Thats what we call snobbery.

LIZA. You dont call the like of them my friends now, I

should hope. Theyve took it out of me often enough with their ridicule when they had the chance; and now I mean to get a bit of my own back. But if I'm to have fashionable clothes, I'll wait. I should like to have some. Mrs Pearce says youre going to give me some to wear in bed at night different to what I wear in the daytime; but it do seem a waste of money when you could get something to shew. Besides, I never could fancy changing into cold things on a winter night.

MRS PEARCE [*coming back*] Now, Eliza. The new things have come for you to try on.

LIZA. Ah-ow-oo-ooh! [*She rushes out*].

MRS PEARCE [*following her*] Oh, dont rush about like that, girl. [*She shuts the door behind her*].

HIGGINS. Pickering: we have taken on a stiff job.

PICKERING [*with conviction*] Higgins: we have.

   *   *   *   *   *   *

There seems to be some curiosity as to what Higgins's lessons to Eliza were like. Well, here is a sample: the first one.

Picture Eliza, in her new clothes, and feeling her inside put out of step by a lunch, dinner, and breakfast of a kind to which it is unaccustomed, seated with Higgins and the Colonel in the study, feeling like a hospital out-patient at a first encounter with the doctors.

Higgins, constitutionally unable to sit still, discomposes her still more by striding restlessly about. But for the reassuring presence and quietude of her friend the Colonel she would run for her life, even back to Drury Lane.

HIGGINS. Say your alphabet.

LIZA. I know my alphabet. Do you think I know nothing? I dont need to be taught like a child.

HIGGINS [*thundering*] Say your alphabet.

PICKERING. Say it, Miss Doolittle. You will understand presently. Do what he tells you; and let him teach you in his own way.

LIZA. Oh well, if you put it like that—Ahyee, bəyee, cəyee, dəyee—

HIGGINS [*with the roar of a wounded lion*] Stop. Listen to this, Pickering. This is what we pay for as elementary education. This unfortunate animal has been locked up for nine years in school at our expense to teach her to speak and read the language of Shakespear and Milton. And the result is

Ahyee, Bə-yee, Cə-yee, Dəyee. [*To Eliza*] Say A, B, C, D.

LIZA [*almost in tears*] But I'm sayin it. Ahyee, Bəyee, Cə-yee—

HIGGINS. Stop. Say a cup of tea.

LIZA. A cappətə-ee.

HIGGINS. Put your tongue forward until it squeezes against the top of your lower teeth. Now say cup.

LIZA. C-c-c—I cant. C-Cup.

PICKERING. Good. Splendid, Miss Doolittle.

HIGGINS. By Jupiter, she's done it the first shot. Pickering: we shall make a duchess of her. [*To Eliza*] Now do you think you could possibly say tea? Not tə-yee, mind: if you ever say bə-yee cə-yee də-yee again you shall be dragged round the room three times by the hair of your head. [*Fortissimo*] T, T, T, T.

LIZA [*weeping*] I cant hear no difference cep that it sounds more genteel-like when you say it.

HIGGINS. Well, if you can hear that difference, what the devil are you crying for? Pickering: give her a chocolate.

PICKERING. No, no. Never mind crying a little, Miss Doolittle: you are doing very well; and the lessons wont hurt. I promise you I wont let him drag you round the room by your hair.

HIGGINS. Be off with you to Mrs Pearce and tell her about it. Think about it. Try to do it by yourself: and keep your tongue well forward in your mouth instead of trying to roll it up and swallow it. Another lesson at half-past four this afternoon. Away with you.

Eliza, still sobbing, rushes from the room.

And that is the sort of ordeal poor Eliza has to go through for months before we meet her again on her first appearance in London society of the professional class.

PYGMALION

— • • —

ACT III

ACT III

It is Mrs Higgins's at-home day. Nobody has yet arrived. Her drawing room, in a flat on Chelsea Embankment, has three windows looking on the river; and the ceiling is not so lofty as it would be in an older house of the same pretension. The windows are open, giving access to a balcony with flowers in pots. If you stand with your face to the windows, you have the fireplace on your left and the door in the right-hand wall close to the corner nearest the windows.

Mrs Higgins was brought up on Morris and Burne Jones; and her room, which is very unlike her son's room in Wimpole Street, is not crowded with furniture and little tables and nicknacks. In the middle of the room there is a big ottoman; and this, with the carpet, the Morris wall-papers, and the Morris chintz window curtains and brocade covers of the ottoman and its cushions, supply all the ornament, and are much too handsome to be hidden by odds and ends of useless things. A few good oil-paintings from the exhibitions in the Grosvenor Gallery thirty years ago (the Burne Jones, not the Whistler side of them) are on the walls. The only landscape is a Cecil Lawson on the scale of a Rubens. There is a portrait of Mrs Higgins as she was when she defied the fashion in her youth in one of the beautiful Rossettian costumes which, when caricatured by people who did not understand, led to the absurdities of popular estheticism in the eighteen-seventies.

In the corner diagonally opposite the door Mrs Higgins, now over sixty and long past taking the trouble to dress out

*of the fashion, sits writing at an elegantly simple writing-
table with a bell button within reach of her hand. There is a
Chippendale chair further back in the room between her and
the window nearest her side. At the other side of the room,
further forward, is an Elizabethan chair roughly carved in the
taste of Inigo Jones. On the same side a piano in a decorated
case. The corner between the fireplace and the window is
occupied by a divan cushioned in Morris chintz.*

It is between four and five in the afternoon.

*The door is opened violently; and Higgins enters with his
hat on.*

MRS HIGGINS [*dismayed*] Henry! [*Scolding him*] What are
you doing here today? It is my at-home day: you promised
not to come. [*As he bends to kiss her, she takes his hat off,
and presents it to him*].

HIGGINS. Oh bother! [*He throws the hat down on the table*].

MRS HIGGINS. Go home at once.

HIGGINS [*kissing her*] I know, mother. I came on purpose.

MRS HIGGINS. But you mustnt. I'm serious, Henry. You
offend all my friends: they stop coming whenever they meet
you.

HIGGINS. Nonsense! I know I have no small talk; but people
dont mind. [*He sits on the settee*].

MRS HIGGINS. Oh! dont they? Small talk indeed! What about
your large talk? Really, dear, you mustnt stay.

HIGGINS. I must. Ive a job for you. A phonetic job.

MRS HIGGINS. No use, dear. I'm sorry; but I cant get round
your vowels; and though I like to get pretty postcards in your
patent shorthand, I always have to read the copies in ordinary
writing you so thoughtfully send me.

HIGGINS. Well, this isnt a phonetic job.

MRS HIGGINS. You said it was.

HIGGINS. Not your part of it. Ive picked up a girl.

MRS HIGGINS. Does that mean that some girl has picked you
up?

HIGGINS. Not at all. I dont mean a love affair.

MRS HIGGINS. What a pity!

HIGGINS. Why?

MRS HIGGINS. Well, you never fall in love with anyone under forty-five. When will you discover that there are some
rather nice-looking young women about?

HIGGINS. Oh, I cant be bothered with young women. My idea of a lovable woman is somebody as like you as possible. I shall never get into the way of seriously liking young women: some habits lie too deep to be changed. [*Rising abruptly and walking about, jingling his money and his keys in his trouser pockets*] Besides, theyre all idiots.

MRS HIGGINS. Do you know what you would do if you really loved me, Henry?

HIGGINS. Oh bother! What? Marry, I suppose.

MRS HIGGINS. No. Stop fidgeting and take your hands out of your pockets. [*With a gesture of despair, he obeys and sits down again*]. Thats a good boy. Now tell me about the girl.

HIGGINS. She's coming to see you.

MRS HIGGINS. I dont remember asking her.

HIGGINS. You didnt. *I* asked her. If youd known her you wouldnt have asked her.

MRS HIGGINS. Indeed! Why?

HIGGINS. Well, it's like this. She's a common flower girl. I picked her off the kerbstone.

MRS HIGGINS. And invited her to my at-home!

HIGGINS [*rising and coming to her to coax her*] Oh, thatll be all right. Ive taught her to speak properly; and she has strict orders as to her behavior. She's to keep to two subjects: the weather and everybody's health—Fine day and How do you do, you know—and not to let herself go on things in general. That will be safe.

MRS HIGGINS. Safe! To talk about our health! about our insides! perhaps about our outsides! How could you be so silly, Henry?

HIGGINS [*impatiently*] Well, she must talk about something. [*He controls himself and sits down again*]. Oh, she'll be all right: dont you fuss. Pickering is in it with me. Ive a sort of bet on that I'll pass her off as a duchess in six months. I started on her some months ago; and she's getting on like a house on fire. I shall win my bet. She has a quick ear; and she's easier to teach than my middle-class pupils because she's had to learn a complete new language. She talks English almost as you talk French.

MRS HIGGINS. Thats satisfactory, at all events.

HIGGINS. Well, it is and it isnt.

MRS HIGGINS. What does that mean?

HIGGINS. You see, Ive got her pronunciation all right; but

you have to consider not only how a girl pronounces, but what she pronounces; and thats where—

They are interrupted by the parlor-maid, announcing guests.

THE PARLOR-MAID. Mrs and Miss Eynsford Hill. [*She withdraws*].

HIGGINS. Oh Lord! [*He rises; snatches his hat from the table; and makes for the door; but before he reaches it his mother introduces him*].

Mrs and Miss Eynsford Hill are the mother and daughter who sheltered from the rain in Covent Garden. The mother is well bred, quiet, and has the habitual anxiety of straitened means. The daughter has acquired a gay air of being very much at home in society: the bravado of genteel poverty.

MRS EYNSFORD HILL [*to Mrs Higgins*] How do you do? [*They shake hands*].

MISS EYNSFORD HILL. How d'you do? [*She shakes*].

MRS HIGGINS [*introducing*] My son Henry.

MRS EYNSFORD HILL. Your celebrated son! I have so longed to meet you, Professor Higgins.

HIGGINS [*glumly, making no movement in her direction*] Delighted. [*He backs against the piano and bows brusquely*].

MISS EYNSFORD HILL [*going to him with confident familiarity*] How do you do?

HIGGINS [*staring at her*] Ive seen you before somewhere. I havnt the ghost of a notion where; but Ive heard your voice. [*Drearily*] It doesnt matter. Youd better sit down.

MRS HIGGINS. I'm sorry to say that my celebrated son has no manners. You mustnt mind him.

MISS EYNSFORD HILL [*gaily*] I dont. [*She sits in the Elizabethan chair*].

MRS EYNSFORD HILL [*a little bewildered*] Not at all. [*She sits on the ottoman between her daughter and Mrs Higgins, who has turned her chair away from the writing-table*].

HIGGINS. Oh, have I been rude? I didnt mean to be.

He goes to the central window, through which, with his back to the company, he contemplates the river and the flowers in Battersea Park on the opposite bank as if they were a frozen desert.

The parlor-maid returns, ushering in Pickering.

THE PARLOR-MAID. Colonel Pickering. [*She withdraws*].

PICKERING. How do you do, Mrs Higgins?

MRS HIGGINS. So glad youve come. Do you know Mrs Eynsford Hill—Miss Eynsford Hill? [*Exchange of bows. The Colonel brings the Chippendale chair a little forward between Mrs Hill and Mrs Higgins, and sits down*].

PICKERING. Has Henry told you what weve come for?

HIGGINS [*over his shoulder*] We were interrupted: damn it!

MRS HIGGINS. Oh Henry, Henry, really!

MRS EYNSFORD HILL [*half rising*] Are we in the way?

MRS HIGGINS [*rising and making her sit down again*] No, no. You couldnt have come more fortunately: we want you to meet a friend of ours.

HIGGINS [*turning hopefully*] Yes, by George! We want two or three people. Youll do as well as anybody else.

The parlor-maid returns, ushering Freddy.

THE PARLOR-MAID. Mr Eynsford Hill.

HIGGINS [*almost audibly, past endurance*] God of Heaven! another of them.

FREDDY [*shaking hands with Mrs Higgins*] Ahdedo?

MRS HIGGINS. Very good of you to come. [*Introducing*] Colonel Pickering.

FREDDY [*bowing*] Ahdedo?

MRS HIGGINS. I dont think you know my son, Professor Higgins.

FREDDY [*going to Higgins*] Ahdedo?

HIGGINS [*looking at him much as if he were a pickpocket*] I'll take my oath Ive met you before somewhere. Where was it?

FREDDY. I dont think so.

HIGGINS [*resignedly*] It dont matter, anyhow. Sit down.

He shakes Freddy's hand, and almost slings him on to the ottoman with his face to the window; then comes round to the other side of it.

HIGGINS. Well, here we are, anyhow! [*He sits down on the ottoman next Mrs Eynsford Hill, on her left*] And now, what the devil are we going to talk about until Eliza comes?

MRS HIGGINS. Henry: you are the life and soul of the Royal Society's soirées; but really youre rather trying on more commonplace occasions.

HIGGINS. Am I? Very sorry. [*Beaming suddenly*] I suppose I am, you know. [*Uproariously*] Ha, ha!

MISS EYNSFORD HILL [*who considers Higgins quite eligible matrimonially*] I sympathize. I havnt any small talk. If people would only be frank and say what they really think!

HIGGINS [*relapsing into gloom*] Lord forbid!

MRS EYNSFORD HILL [*taking up her daughter's cue*] But why?

HIGGINS. What they think they ought to think is bad enough, Lord knows; but what they really think would break up the whole show. Do you suppose it would be really agreeable if I were to come out now with what *I* really think?

MISS EYNSFORD HILL [*gaily*] Is it so very cynical?

HIGGINS. Cynical! Who the dickens said it was cynical? I mean it wouldnt be decent.

MRS EYNSFORD HILL [*seriously*] Oh! I'm sure you dont mean that, Mr Higgins.

HIGGINS. You see, we're all savages, more or less. We're supposed to be civilized and cultured—to know all about poetry and philosophy and art and science, and so on; but how many of us know even the meanings of these names? [*To Miss Hill*] What do you know of poetry? [*To Mrs Hill*] What do you know of science? [*Indicating Freddy*] What does he know of art or science or anything else? What the devil do you imagine I know of philosophy?

MRS HIGGINS [*warningly*] Or of manners, Henry?

THE PARLOR-MAID [*opening the door*] Miss Doolittle. [*She withdraws*].

HIGGINS [*rising hastily and running to Mrs Higgins*] Here she is, mother. [*He stands on tiptoe and makes signs over his mother's head to Eliza to indicate to her which lady is her hostess*].

Eliza, who is exquisitely dressed, produces an impression of such remarkable distinction and beauty as she enters that they all rise, quite fluttered. Guided by Higgins's signals, she comes to Mrs Higgins with studied grace.

LIZA [*speaking with pedantic correctness of pronunciation and great beauty of tone*] How do you do, Mrs Higgins? [*She gasps slightly in making sure of the H in Higgins, but is quite successful*]. Mr Higgins told me I might come.

MRS HIGGINS [*cordially*] Quite right: I'm very glad indeed to see you.

PICKERING. How do you do, Miss Doolittle?

LIZA [*shaking hands with him*] Colonel Pickering, is it not?

MRS EYNSFORD HILL. I feel sure we have met before, Miss Doolittle. I remember your eyes.

Reader's Supplement

to

PYGMALION

GEORGE BERNARD SHAW (1856–1950)

BIOGRAPHICAL BACKGROUND

The central idea of *Pygmalion* and the character of Henry Higgins were the result of Shaw's lifelong interest in phonetics, shorthand, and reformed spelling, an interest which began before he was twenty and lasted until his death at the age of ninety-four. Convinced that the English alphabet of twenty-six letters did not represent accurately all the sounds of the language, he devised what he called a New Alphabet, in which each letter stood for one sound and one sound only. Throughout the years, he appealed to the government, colleges, trusts, and societies to sponsor his New Alphabet. After all his efforts had failed, he decided to empower the executors of his will to use the bulk of his considerable estate to finance "any promising scheme for providing a new phonetic alphabet capable of expressing the forty-two sounds listed by the late Henry Sweet, Oxford Reader of Phonetics, and then publishing and depositing in the leading libraries certain English classics transliterated into the said alphabet."

Because he doubted that his plan would be carried out, his will contained the alternate instructions that, if his favorite scheme were found impossible, the bulk of his estate should be divided among the National Gallery of Ireland, which had initiated his knowledge of art; the British Museum, which had served as his library and club for years; and the Royal Academy of Dramatic Art, as a remembrance to the actors in his many plays. The will was disputed at law and found impractical. The result was that his three favorite institutions benefited from his fortune, by that time greatly increased by the huge royalties from the musical play and film, *My Fair Lady,* based on his *Pygmalion.*

George Bernard Shaw was born in Dublin, Ireland, on

July 26, 1856. He left school at fifteen and became a junior clerk in a land agent's office. He hated the office work, although he quickly rose to a senior position with responsibility far beyond his years. He was influenced during this time by the friendship of Chichester Bell, a cousin of the inventor of the telephone and a nephew of Alexander Melville Bell, who had invented a phonetic script called Visible Speech.

At twenty, Shaw left Dublin and went to London. There followed ten years of poverty, Shaw spending much of his time reading in the British Museum. He was determined to write but found that no one would publish his novels. During this time, his writing brought him only about thirty dollars, most of which came in payment for a patent medicine advertisement. He gave up trying to be a novelist and became a newspaper critic, first of music, then of art, and later of the theatre. In his dramatic criticism, Shaw attacked the fashionable, artificial plays of the time, championed Ibsen's dramas of ideas and social problems, and paved the way for his own plays.

Shaw's acquaintances during these years greatly influenced his ideas and his work. He met Lecky, Ellis, and Sweet, all of whom were deeply interested in phonetics. In his preface to *Pygmalion* (pp. vii–xii), Shaw paid tribute to Henry Sweet and acknowledged touches of Sweet in the portrait of Henry Higgins. Deeply interested in socialism, Shaw met Sydney Webb, with whom he greatly influenced the Fabian Society, an organization whose purpose was to debate and disseminate the truth about the relations between the social classes. Together Shaw and Webb developed England's Liberal Party and later helped form the Labour Party. In order to make known his theories of social reform, Shaw became an accomplished speaker, propagandist, and pamphleteer.

Success came slowly to Shaw. Theatre managers refused his plays for years; instead of the usual situations and sentiments common to the stage, Shaw gave them social satire, unconventional philosophy, and intellectual dialogue. For years, critics complained that he did not write for the stage but used the theatre as others might use the newspaper, pulpit, or lecture platform. Finally, his plays became a vogue. Critics and public alike acclaimed his wit and satire, his comic scenes and characters, his good-humored but sincere ideas, and his mixture of fun with philosophy.

A vegetarian, teetotaler, and nonsmoker, Shaw worked hard and lived simply. At last a literary celebrity, he refused many high honors offered to him. He was awarded the Nobel Prize for Literature in 1925, accepted the honor, but declined the money award that attended it. Visitors to his home at Ayot St. Lawrence were frequently amused to notice that Shaw, who was supposedly not interested in awards, kept on prominent display in his study the Oscar he had won for the film version of *Pygmalion*. On his ninetieth birthday, swarms of people visited his home as though it were a shrine. He died on November 2, 1950.

During his long life, Shaw made many famous friends, who were attracted by his never-failing wit, good humor, vitality, curiosity, and maddening self-assurance. He met his match with one such friend, Winston Churchill. Shaw sent Churchill tickets for the opening night of *Pygmalion* with this note attached: "I enclose two tickets for the first night of my new play, one for yourself and one for your friend—if you have one." Churchill returned the tickets with this reply: "I am sorry I cannot attend for the first night of *Pygmalion,* but I should be glad to come on the second night—if there is one."

Note: The page references on the following pages direct your attention to passages in the text (T for Top of page, M for Middle, and B for Bottom).

HISTORICAL BACKGROUND

According to Ovid's *Metamorphoses,* Pygmalion was a king of Cyprus and a sculptor. He created a statue of a woman so beautiful that he fell in love with it and prayed to Aphrodite to give him a wife resembling the statue he had made. Aphrodite heard his prayer and brought the statue to life so that Pygmalion might marry her. The story was later used in John Marston's poem, *The Metamorphosis of Pygmalion's Image,* in William Morris's *The Earthly Paradise,* and in W. S. Gilbert's comedy, *Pygmalion and Galatea.* Shaw decided to use *Pygmalion* as the title of his play about the transformation of a ragged Cockney girl, but he was careful to insist that the hero did not fall in love with his creation.

For his setting, Shaw used London in the first dozen years of the twentieth century. Automobiles, the motor bus, and motorized taxicabs had been introduced, but many elegant families still retained their coachmen and carriages (p. 92B). People believed that rigid class distinctions should be observed. Although the boys of rich families might be educated for the professions, those of inherited wealth still believed themselves superior to those who earned money in business or "trade," as they called it. Even in families (such as the Eynsford-Hills) in which the inherited wealth had dwindled to the extent that it could no longer support a life of ease and luxury, there was little thought of training the children for gainful employment. Instead, they tried to live like the money classes and busied themselves, as did people of greater wealth, in activities such as attending concerts, the theatre, exhibitions, and any "at-home" afternoons, formal dinners, garden parties, and receptions to which they could manage to be invited. Rich women dressed in voluminous clothing and favored an overabundance of household decoration. There was little freedom and ease in social relations, and the upper classes showed reticence toward considering the problems of life and toward facing unpleasant facts. It was against the snobbery of wealthy society that Shaw directed his satire. He delighted in mocking social shams and conventionalities. Through Liza he set out to prove that high society with its artificial standards could be deluded into thinking her a duchess or a princess merely because of her appearance, dress, and speech.

In contrast to the life of the wealthy, Shaw depicted the meager existence of the poor. While conditions had greatly improved for the working classes, the poor had few advantages. Nine years of elementary schooling were provided at public expense (p. 42B), but Liza's speech showed how ineffectual that schooling was. She made her living by selling flowers on the street, but her vulgar speech barred her from securing a position in a flower shop. Her slum dwelling provided no heat or hot water, and light was available only by putting coins into a slot meter (p. 14T). She had never had a bath in her life (p. 29T) and had never heard of wearing nightclothes (p. 29M) other than underwear. Like many girls of her station in life, she had been put out of her home to earn her own living soon after completing her required schooling. Public assistance was available to those whom her father called "the deserving poor" (p. 38T), but he complained that he, as a member of "the undeserving poor," got no assistance and had to make his living and get money for drink and amusements by his efforts as a garbage-collector and by inducing others to give him money (p. 84B).

Household servants, of course, were in a different category. Like the salespeople in fine shops, they had to speak acceptably in order to deal with their employers and the visitors in the house. That a housekeeper might be so bold as to criticize her employer was evident in Mrs. Pearce's reminders to Professor Higgins about his table-manners and his swearing (pp. 32T–33T).

A matter of what is by now mainly of historical interest is the use of the word *bloody*. When Liza said "Not bloody likely!" (p. 55M), she created a sensation in Mrs. Higgins's drawing room and in early theatrical performances of the play, as well. It was exactly that word which Mrs. Pearce implored Professor Higgins not to use in Liza's hearing (p. 32T). As the years passed, however, the word began gradually to lose its capacity to shock people.

Shaw had observed that, when his plays were first performed in London, they were rather coolly received by the critics and by the public. Success on foreign stages, however, made his English critics less caustic when the plays finally reached London. Accordingly, he decided to have *Pygmalion* performed first in the German language. It was a success in Vienna in 1913 and also in Berlin. By the time it was presented in London in 1914, it was highly successful and has remained popular ever since. *Pygmalion* as a film gave the play a wider audience. Its popularity was vastly increased by the musical play and subsequent motion picture, *My Fair Lady*. It gave thorough delight to its audiences even though critics doubt that Shaw, had he lived to see it, would have approved the musical version and particularly its happy ending.

PICTORIAL BACKGROUND

The Daughter [in the space between the central pillars, close to the one on her left] *I'm getting chilled to the bone. What can Freddy be doing all this time? He's been gone twenty minutes.*

The Mother [on her daughter's right] *Not so long. But he ought to have got us a cab by this.* (p. 3M)

THE PILLARS IN COVENT GARDEN MARKET—LATE 1800's

The Daughter. *No. Ive nothing smaller than sixpence.*

The Flower Girl [hopefully] *I can give you change for a tanner, kind lady.*

The Mother [to Clara] *Give it to me.* [Clara parts reluctantly]. *Now* [to the girl] *this is for your flowers.*

The Flower Girl. *Thank you kindly, lady. (p. 5M)*

LONDON FLOWER GIRL—LATE 1800's

The Flower Girl. *Let him mind his own business and leave a poor girl—*

The Note Taker [explosively] *Woman: cease this detestable boohooing instantly; or else seek the shelter of some other place of worship.*

The Flower Girl [with feeble defiance] *Ive a right to be here if I like, same as you.* (p. 11T)

HIGGINS AND LIZA IN COVENT GARDEN.
(*From My Fair Lady with permission of Warner Brothers*)

Higgins. *I was going to India to meet you.*

    Pickering. *Where do you live?*

    Higgins. *27A Wimpole Street. Come and see me to-morrow.*

    Pickering. *I'm at the Carlton. Come with me now and lets have a jaw over some supper. (p. 12T)*

BACK VIEW OF HOUSES ON WIMPOLE STREET, LONDON

Freddy [springing out of a taxicab] *Got one at last. Hallo!* [To the girl] *Where are the two ladies that were here?*

The Flower Girl. *They walked to the bus when the rain stopped.*

Freddy. *And left me with a cab on my hands! Damnation!*

The Flower Girl [with grandeur] *Never mind, young man. I'm going home in a taxi. (p. 12B)*

LOOKING FOR TAXIS ON A RAINY NIGHT
IN LONDON—EARLY 1900's

She picks up the basket and trudges up the alley with it to her lodging: a small room with very old wall paper hanging loose in the damp places. A broken pane in the window is mended with paper. A portrait of a popular actor and a fashion plate of ladies' dresses, all wildly beyond poor Liza's means, both torn from newspapers, are pinned up on the wall. (p. 13B)

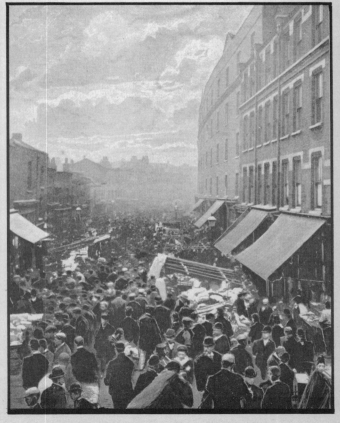

A STREET IN THE POOR SECTION OF LONDON

Mrs Pearce. *Nonsense. Here: step in and tell me whether it's hot enough for you.*

Liza. *Ah-oo! Ah-oo! It's too hot.*

Mrs Pearce [deftly snatching the gown away and throwing Liza down on her back] *It wont hurt you.* [She sets to work with the scrubbing brush]. *(p. 30T)*

BATHROOM—EARLY 1900's

Higgins. *Put your tongue forward until it squeezes against the top of your lower teeth. Now say cup.*

Liza. *C-c-c—I cant. C-Cup.*

Pickering. *Good. Splendid, Miss Doolittle.*

Higgins. *By Jupiter, she's done it the first shot. Pickering: we shall make a duchess of her. (p. 43T)*

A MOMENT OF TRIUMPH FOR THE PROFESSOR AND HIS PUPIL
(From My Fair Lady *with permission of Warner Brothers)*

Eliza, who is exquisitely dressed, produces an impression of such remarkable distinction and beauty as she enters that they all rise, quite fluttered. Guided by Higgins's signals, she comes to Mrs Higgins with studied grace.

Liza [speaking with pedantic correctness of pronunciation and great beauty of tone] *How do you do, Mrs Higgins? (p. 52B)*

A WELL-TURNED-OUT YOUNG LADY—1900

Mrs Higgins [at last, conversationally] *Will it rain, do you think?*

Liza. *The shallow depression in the west of these islands is likely to move slowly in an easterly direction. There are no indications of any great change in the barometrical situation. (p. 53M)*

LIZA SHOWS OFF HER NEWLY ACQUIRED CULTURE DURING AT-HOME TEA WITH THE MOTHER OF PROFESSOR HIGGINS
(*From* My Fair Lady *with permission of Warner Brothers*)

As is customary in adaptation of books or plays for motion picture treatment, scenes are often added to flesh out the details of the plot or to introduce variety in the background. In My Fair Lady, *Liza (Audrey Hepburn) spends a day at the Ascot Races in the company of Professor Higgins (Rex Harrison) and Colonel Pickering (Wilfrid Hyde-White).*

A NECESSARY INGREDIENT IN
LIZA'S MOUNTING SOPHISTICATION
(*From* My Fair Lady *with permission of Warner Brothers*)

Pickering [to Eliza] *Now, ready?*

    Liza. *Ready.*

    Pickering. *Go.*

    They mount the stairs, Higgins last. Pickering whispers to the footman on the first landing.

    First Landing Footman. *Miss Doolittle, Colonel Pickering, Professor Higgins. (p. 62B)*

AN ELEGANT RECEPTION—LATE 1800's

At the top of the staircase the Ambassador and his wife, with Nepommuck at her elbow, are receiving.

Hostess [taking Liza's hand] *How d'ye do?*

Host [same play] *How d'ye do? How d'ye do, Pickering?*

Liza [with a beautiful gravity that awes her hostess] *How do you do?* [She passes on to the drawingroom]. *(p. 63T)*

LIZA CREATING A SENSATION AT THE EMBASSY RECEPTION
(From *My Fair Lady* *with permission of Warner Brothers*)

Liza. *I heard your prayers. "Thank God it's all over!"*

Higgins [impatiently] *Well, dont you thank God it's all over? Now you are free and can do what you like.*

Liza [pulling herself together in desperation] *What am I fit for? What have you left me fit for? Where am I to go? What am I to do? Whats to become of me?* (p. 73M)

AFTER THE BALL IS OVER . . .
(*From My Fair Lady with permission of Warner Brothers*)

Doolittle enters. He is resplendently dressed as for a fashionable wedding and might, in fact, be the bridegroom. A flower in his buttonhole, a dazzling silk hat, and patent leather shoes complete the effect. He is too concerned with the business he has come on to notice Mrs Higgins. He walks straight to Higgins, and accosts him with vehement reproach. (p. 83T)

A GENTLEMAN "RESPLENDENTLY DRESSED"

Another scene added in the motion picture treatment of Pygmalion is one in which Liza, having renounced Professor Higgins, is courted by Freddy. Here, in My Fair Lady, the poor fellow suffers a slight mishap, thereby symbolically fulfilling Shaw's statement, in his epilogue to the play (p. 104M): "Weak people want to marry strong people who do not frighten them...."

HEAD OVER HEELS ...
(From My Fair Lady with permission of Warner Brothers)

And so it came about that Eliza's luck held, and the expected opposition to the flower shop melted away. The shop is in the arcade of a railway station not very far from the Victoria and Albert Museum; and if you live in that neighbourhood you may go there any day and buy a buttonhole from Eliza. (p. 109B)

LONDON RAILWAY STATION

LITERARY ALLUSIONS AND NOTES

crying in the wilderness (p. viiB):
This is a somewhat oblique reference to John the Baptist: "I am the voice of one crying in the wilderness," *John* I:23. Similarly, in his Afterword Shaw refers to the contemporary novelist H. G. Wells in terms that Shakespeare used to describe the Queen of the Nile in his *Antony and Cleopatra:* "Age had not yet withered him, nor could custom stale his infinite variety"—and then Shaw adds mischievously "in half an hour."

Ibsen or Samuel Butler (p. viiiT):
Both the Norwegian playwright Henrik Ibsen (1828–1906) and the English novelist *(The Way of All Flesh)* Samuel Butler (1835–1902) were very unconciliatory when it came to evils they perceived in bourgeois society —and both had immense impact upon Shaw.

Joseph Chamberlain (p. viiiT):
This British statesman (1836–1914) was probably better known for his leadership of the Radicals (tax reforms, free schools, creation of allotments by compulsory purchase, etc.) than for his brilliant administration as secretary for the colonies under the Coalition government.

Clarendon Press (p. ixT):
The press of Oxford University is named for its benefactor, Edward Hyde, first Earl of Clarendon (1608–1674).

Pitman (p. ixB) and Gregg (p. xM):
Sir Isaac Pitman (1813–1897) was a leader in phonetics, spelling reform, and shorthand *(Stenographic Sound Hand,* 1837), and was followed by John Robert Gregg (1867–1942) who invented a system of shorthand (1888) which rapidly caught on in America and elsewhere.

alphabet . . . Russian size (p. xM):
The Cyrillic alphabet used for Russian and other Slavonic languages involved the invention of extra signs for sounds not covered by the Greek alphabet from which the two Slavonic alphabets (Cyrillic and Glagolitic) were devel-

oped in the ninth century. Shaw was in favor of a much extended alphabet for writing English more accurately and left large sums in his will for the cause.

Thames (p. xB):
The river that runs through London (pronounced "Tems"). The proverbial expression "to set a river on fire" means to accomplish the impossible and gain reknown.

Robert Bridges (p. xiT):
This English poet (1844–1930), who published his masterpiece *The Testament of Beauty* on his eighty-fifth birthday after years in retirement, was a leading exponent of spelling reform and a notable critic of Milton's prosody, "to whom perhaps," writes Shaw, "Higgins may owe his Miltonic sympathies."

Ruy Blas **(p. xiB):**
In this play by Victor Hugo (1802–1885), written in 1838, a valet falls in love with a queen. To play the queen's role at the prestigious national theatre (Théâtre Français) was long the goal of aspiring actresses.

an e upside down (p. xiiB):
In phonetics this weak neutral vowel (the *a* in *alone*, the *u* in *circus*) is called a *schwa*. Shaw's care with the dialect throughout the play is remarkable, though he abandons "this desperate attempt to represent her dialect without a phonetic alphabet" after Eliza's first speech. (That speech, by the way, on p. 5M, in "English" is: *Oh, he's your son, is he? Well, if you had done your duty by him as a mother should, he would know better than to spoil a poor girl's flowers then run away without paying. Will you pay me for them?*)

Covent Garden (p. 3T):
London's vegetable and flower market (now being demolished) stands near the famous Theatre Royal in Drury Lane and the Theatre Royal, Covent Garden (an opera house). One of the landmarks of the area is the church designed by Inigo Jones (1573–1652), who laid out the areas of Covent Garden and Lincoln's Inn Fields.

I'm getting chilled (p. 3M):
Shaw had his own eccentric ideas about spelling (in ad-

dition to rendering *show* as *shew* in the old-fashioned way) and on the very first page we are brought up short by the inconsistency of putting the apostrophe into *I'm* and *it's* and leaving it out of *aint* and *couldnt*. Throughout the play we shall see words like *arnt* (p. 91T) and *maam* (p. 81T).

Charing Cross (p. 4T):

This railway station site in London and the other places mentioned suggest that Freddy has been far-ranging in search of a cab. "Strandwards" means "toward the Strand," a street in London which (as its name suggests) was long ago the beach alongside the river Thames.

tanner (p. 5M):

Sixpence (about 12¢, then). Other coins mentioned are a *shilling* (about 25¢, then), a *florin* (two shillings), *half-a-crown* (two shillings and sixpence), etc. The *sovereign* (a gold coin then in use) and the *guinea* (even then long out of use as an actual coin) also figure in the play. British money having changed in the 1970's, in time these words may require as much explanation for Shaw's countrymen as they do today for Americans.

bloke (p. 6B):

Cockney slang for "fellow." Other examples abound in the play, such as *copper's nark* (p. 7M), which even Higgins, oddly, doesn't seem to know means "informer for the police"; *jaw* (p. 12T), which means "chat," perhaps here of public school origin; *off his chump* and *balmies* (p. 24M), "crazy" and "crazy people"; *copper* (p. 28B), used here to mean "washtub"; *Governor* (p. 34T), a term of respect, usually abbreviated to *Guv* and equivalent to "sir"; etc. Shaw is usually careful that the meaning of slang words is clear in the context, whether familiar or not (example: *tec,* p. 8T), though any Englishman in his audience would know these.

charge (p. 7T):

As used here, the word means "arrest" (charge with a crime); *navvy* (p. 41B) means "ditch-digger" or some other kind of manual laborer; and *fender* (p. 53M) is a rail around the fireplace hearth, not something on a car.

As Shaw said, Britain and America are two countries separated by a common language.

Lisson Grove (p. 8M):
This poor section of London reveals that Liza is both from the slums and, at Covent Garden, "far east" from her home. The social class of people from other locations (Selsey; Hoxton; Earl's Court, which Shaw insists on rendering as one word; Epsom, famous for the horse races held there; Tottenham Court Road; Chelsea Embankment, a very fashionable "artistic" neighborhood, and Battersea, just across the river but light years away in the social scale) would be immediately obvious to snobbish Londoners, just as "Nob Hill" would mean "upper-class" to San Franciscans, "Bowery" would "place" someone in New York, etc.

Housing Question (p. 8M):
A popular political talking point then—and now: the housing of the poor, high rents, overcrowding, etc. The speaker says he can't live on Park Lane, London's equivalent of the most "posh" (upper-class and expensive) address in other cities.

Cheltenham, Harrow, Cambridge, and India (p. 9T):
Colonel Pickering's background is instantly sketched by this list of his public schools, his university, and mention of his service in the Indian Army in the days of the British *Raj* there. When we discover (p. 12T) that he is staying at the Carlton Hotel, his money as well as his social class is established. But to Higgins his accent tells all.

Pharisaic (p. 12M):
Pertaining to the Pharisees, a Jewish sect that aroused the anger of Christ because of their strict adherence to the Law of Moses but not its spirit; self-righteous and hypocritical.

best love from all at home (p. 13B):
The Cockney taxi driver tosses off a catch phrase obviously derived from postcard sentiments and intended to be flip.

laryngoscope (p. 17T):
A medical instrument for examining the vocal chords in

the larynx of the throat. Professor Higgins may not have "hi-fi"—he's still using the old phonograph with "wax cylinders," rather like early dictaphones—but Shaw wants to establish him as professional.

Piranesis (p. 18T):
Etchings by Giambattista Piranesi (1720–1778), engraver of Roman antiquities. They help to demonstrate both Higgins's wealth and taste.

Bell's Visible Speech . . . broad Romic (p. 19M):
Professor Higgins refers first to the phonetic system invented by Alexander Melville Bell and then to the less effective Roman alphabet as means of writing down sounds.

stupent (p. 20T):
Latin: "He is astounded!"

Eliza, Elizabeth, Betsy and Bess (p. 21M):
Four names for the same person, which explains the joke of the little children's rhyme Higgins and Pickering recall.

Monkey Brand (p. 23T):
A strong cleaner and polish, the name comes from a trademark of a monkey looking at his reflection in a glass.

officer in the Guards (p. 26B):
An officer in the Household Cavalry, the soldiers that form the royal bodyguard. The point is that officers bought their commissions in these dashing, fashionable regiments and were both wealthy and socially very "eligible" bachelors.

put it in the oven (p. 31M):
Mrs. Pearce suggests this as an effective, though it would be a drastic and probably unsatisfactory, way of sterilizing the straw hat.

begins with the same letter as bath (p. 32T):
Mrs. Pearce is unable to bring herself to repeat the word Eliza used, which was *bloody,* a word the English have always thought exceptionally shocking. (Some etymologists have suggested its bad odor derives from the fact that it is a corruption of a medieval curse, "By your lady," i.e., the Virgin Mary.) Of course there is a "sensation" when Eliza drops the word, like a brick, at the at-home (p. 55M). When *My Fair Lady* was presented another shock-

ing word had to be found as a substitute, for *bloody* shocks no one in America.

mendacity and dishonesty (p. 35T):

Unless we are to imagine that the dramatist wants us to despise Higgins for his bigotry, we must say that Shaw's typically English xenophobia—odd in an Irishman—comes through here. Higgins is saying all Welshmen are thieves, an idea the English cling to and teach their children in the old nursery rhyme:

> *Taffy was a Welshman, Taffy was a thief.*
> *Taffy came to my house and stole a side of beef.*

If it is any comfort to the Welsh, the English are also prejudiced against the Scots, the Irish, the French, the *wogs* (Westernized Oriental Gentlemen), and all the rest of the world. Moreover, Higgins asserts, each class hates all the other classes and identifies its enemies by their accents. Shaw won't even allow Nepommuck (at least at his first appearance, p. 61B) to speak English fluently because he is a Hungarian, though Nepommuck is touted as a master of 32 languages, including the English Professor Higgins taught him. Later on, inconsistently, Nepommuck speaks entirely without such errors as that in "Nobody notice me when I shave" (p. 62T).

at-home day (p. 47T):

Fashionable ladies announced certain days when they were "at home" to casual visitors, who came for tea and a chat. Clara points out that social climbers especially made the rounds of these parties: "we have three at-homes to go to still" (p. 56T). The stiffness and artificiality of these occasions contributes to the fun when Eliza makes her great *gaffe* (social error) by saying the word *bloody* (which she has learned from Professor Higgins).

Morris, Burne-Jones, Grosvenor Gallery, Rosettian (p. 47M and B):

William Morris (1834–1896), craftsman and poet, joined with Sir Edward Burne-Jones (1833–1898), the painter, and Dante Gabriel Rosetti (1828–1882), poet, and painter, to form (with others less important) a Pre-Raphaelite

Brotherhood, both popular and parodied for its esthetic theories and pretensions. Mrs. Higgins's address (Chelsea Embankment, the Rossetti neighborhood, near the house of Oscar Wilde of Tite Street, etc.) and the decoration of her drawing room proclaim her interest, in her youth, in this esthetic movement. The picture "on the scale of Rubens" (big) by Cecil Gordon Lawson (1851–1882), who made his name by exhibiting *The Minister's Garden* at the Grosvenor Gallery in 1878, may show Mrs. Higgins had shocking taste but, at least, a fashionable background in the arts, or on the fringes of them.

some months ago (p. 49B):
Shaw has been writing more of a movie scenario than a play. "Picture Eliza," he says on p. 42M, and then gives us a snatch of scene. Elsewhere in the play, such as the "glimpse" Shaw speaks of at the top of p. 61, we sometimes have the impression of watching a film, not reading a play. On stage, editorial intrusions and unactable stage directions are ignored (or realized in other ways).

Pandour (p. 61B):
Pandours were Croatian infantry in the Austrian Army, noted for their brutality and reckless marauding. In performance, it is hard to see why most of the audience wouldn't think they heard *pander*.

maestro (p. 61B):
People who use the Italian word for *master* in addressing other people—the habit is rife among the more pompous of musicians and singers with resonance where their brains ought to be—cannot escape suggestion of fawning, insincere flattery, or blatant self-importance.

Mrs Langtry (p. 63B):
Emily Charlotte Le Breton (1852–1929), "The Jersey Lily," married Edward Langtry (1874) and was known in the theatre as "Lillie Langtry." She was one of the most beautiful women of her time and a queen of society. People really did stand on their chairs to glimpse her.

Morganatic (p. 64B):
Certain European royal personages were permitted to

contract legitimate marriages with persons of inferior rank (morganatic marriages) provided that titles and estates were not shared by the non-royal person or any descendants of the marriage. Nepommuck means to say that this beautiful "princess" who is only "Miss Doolittle" must be the product of some royal breeding combined with more vigorous and healthy non-royal stock.

speak exactly like Queen Victoria (p. 65T):
One would hope that this intended compliment was not sincere, for Professor Higgins has failed to teach Eliza perfect English if she sounds as Germanic as old Queen Victoria did. Victoria's mother never managed English very well and Victoria's husband, Prince Albert, never conquered the Teutonic tongue with which he was born. Even their son (Edward VII) spoke English like a foreigner

La Fanciulla del Golden West (p. 70T):
Shaw, one of the best music critics in our language, should not have got the title of this opera wrong. It is *La Fanciulla del West* by Giacomo Puccini, from David Belaseo's play *The Girl of the Golden West,* with which Shaw confuses it. The opera was first performed at the Metropolitan Opera House (New York) in 1910, by which time Shaw had long left journalism for drama.

coroneted billet-doux (p. 70M):
A love letter (from the French for "sweet letter") in an envelope from a member of the nobility, bearing a coronet on it. Higgins throws it away unopened as from a "money-lender."

Wimbledon Common (p. 78M):
A park very distant from central London. Obviously Freddy doesn't want to go there particularly and is saying "just drive."

Ezra D. Wannafeller (p. 84M):
A concocted and intentionally funny American name, it is compounded of Wannamaker and Rockefeller, two "titans of industry."

Enry Iggins (p. 85T):
Doolittle seems to be inconsistent in betraying his Cockney origin by dropping his "aitches." On the next page (p.

86M), he can say "Henry" perfectly clearly and at the top of p. 88 he says "Enry Iggins" and "Henry" in one speech after another. An actor might make sense of this by having the "Henry" delivered with care and in obvious imitation of Mrs. Higgins, who of course calls her son "Henry" with no trouble.

Skilly and Char Bydis (pp. 85B and 86T):

Doolittle makes an error in connection with Scylla and Charybdis, the rocks and whirlpool in the Straits of Messina which offered great hazard to navigation: in trying to avoid one the navigator might run into the other.

the moment I entered the room (p. 87T):

The reader (or member of the audience) who recalls the scene will remember that Professor Higgins was not attacked by Eliza either abruptly or without cause, as he seems to forget conveniently, but that poor Eliza was driven to "the point of screaming" before she threw the slippers.

Stilton . . . double Gloucester (p. 99B):

The cheese originally made at Stilton, England, is permeated when ripe with a blue-green mold, which gives it a characteristic sharp flavor. Double Gloucester is a yellow cheese made from double rich milk in Gloucestershire. Anyone who could not tell the difference between them is extremely inattentive or insensitive, and the point being made is that Higgins does not relate to people any better than he does to cheeses: he has his prejudices, but he doesn't notice or feel for reality.

Nell Gwynne (p. 101T):

Eleanor (Nell) Gwynne (c. 1650–1687) is another example of a transformation, a girl of humble parentage who sold oranges at the theatre, became a star at Drury Lane, and progressed from being the mistress of Lord Buckhurst to being the mistress of the king himself, the "merry monarch" Charles II.

Landor (p. 103T):

Walter Savage Landor (1775–1864) was a writer of imposing appearance, iron will, and many gifts, remembered for his *Imaginary Conversations* (1824–1829) and a very few, very touching poems often anthologized.

Nietzsche (p. 103B):
Friedrich Wilhelm Nietzsche (1844–1900) was one of the most influential thinkers of the nineteenth century and his *Also sprach Zarathustra* (1883–1885), developing his idea of the Superman, much colored Shaw's thinking as well as that of others such as Wagner and Hitler.

jointure (p. 104B):
A legal arrangement whereby the wife has during her lifetime the income from a dead husband's estate. Mrs. Eynsford-Hill (and the double name is designed to indicate a certain pretension as well as to avoid the simplicity of "Hill") is described as deriving from a fairly wealthy family (Longlady Park being their seat) but now "in reduced circumstances," as the Victorians used to say to describe shabby gentility or aristocrats down on their luck, what Shaw would call "downstarts."

H. G. Wells (p. 107T):
Herbert George Wells (1866–1946) started life as a draper's apprentice and made himself one of the most popular of English writers, publishing everything from science and science fiction to comic novels and *The Outline of History* (1920). His interest in social justice and his utopian ideals associated him with Bernard Shaw.

General Booth (p. 108M):
William Booth (1829–1912) was the "general" of the Salvation Army which he founded and gave that name in 1878. His wife Catherine (1829–1890) and his daughter Evangeline (1865–1950) were very active in this missionary work. For Shaw's opinion of the Salvation Army, see his play *Major Barbara*.

Gypsy Smith (p. 108M):
Rodney "Gypsy" Smith (1860–1947) was born a gypsy in Epping Forest and became an evangelist, joining William Booth in the Salvation Army. He left it for the Free Church (1882) and preached in America, Australia, and elsewhere.

Galsworthy (p. 108B):
John Galsworthy (1867–1933), a crusading and popular novelist and playwright, documented his times in *The*

Forsyte Saga, now known to millions all over the world through the medium of the television series created by the British Broadcasting Corporation. Like Cethru in his *Inn of Tranquillity* (1912), Galsworthy was accused of endangering "the laws by causing persons to desire to change them," but actually he opened the public's eyes (as he does Clara's in *Pygmalion*) to many injustices and search. Shaw's point is that at the LSE one could learn system than if he had practiced as a lawyer, for which he qualified before turning to writing moralistic and humanitarian novels.

Porson or Bentley (p. 110T):
Richard Porson (1759–1808) and Richard Bentley (1662–1742) were great minds, stupendous classical scholars.

Balbus (p. 110T):
Lucius Cornelius Balbus of the first century B.C. became Roman consul in 40 B.C. under Octavian, being the first foreigner—he was born in what was then called Hispania Ulterior—to hold that high office. Cicero had earlier defended him against the charge of illegally assuming Roman citizenship and it is probably through Cicero's oration *Pro Balbo* that schoolboys like Freddy happened to hear of him.

London School . . . Kew Gardens (p. 110B):
The London School of Economics and Political Science was founded as part of the University of London in 1895. Kew Gardens are officially called the Royal Botanic Gardens but are best known from their location (Kew is in Surrey, just west of London). They began as 9 acres under the patronage of the dowager Princess of Wales (1761) and now constitute 288 acres of plants, trees, museums, hothouses, and laboratories for botanical research. Shaw's point is that at the LSE one could learn all about business and at Kew all about plants, then put the knowledge together to be a very successful florist.

CRITICAL EXCERPTS

So famous a dramatist as George Bernard Shaw has, quite naturally, been the subject of a great many articles, biographies, and volumes of criticism. We have selected some excerpts which should prove challenging to you. We have included page references to *Pygmalion*, indicated in parentheses, so that you can review sample passages to help you decide whether to accept or reject the quoted comments.

1. *In Germany, France, Russia, and Scandinavia, no dramatic author of English speech, save possibly Shakespeare, equals him in popularity. . . . He is a challenging, vital thinker, a keen and fascinating wielder of words, a skilled shaper of story in dramatic mould, a modern critic with a passion for social betterment, who lives up to his belief and is inspirational in his social dream.*

> Richard Burton, *Bernard Shaw, the Man and the Mask*, Henry Holt and Company, 1916.

2. *He performed a definite service in establishing the fact that our stage can be serious in intent . . . without giving up the specific object—to entertain its patrons. It is Shaw's peculiar gift and distinctive service to use the playhouse for serious discussion without being dull. . . . It is not the intellectuals alone who appreciate and applaud him, but the general theatre public, a public caring little or nothing about his reformatory purposes but reacting gladly to his wit and humor, his flair for character, his genius for story and situation. . . . These facts rebut the assertion that Shaw's dramas are not really dramas at all, but stage discussions.*

> Burton, *Bernard Shaw, the Man and the Mask*.

3. *He has been serious. Yet the ordinary opinion of him is*

that he is a clown, a mountebank, a man who has nothing consistent to say and desires only to turn common sense upside down for the mystification or amusement of his audiences. Here he suffers the fate which clear and lively minds have always suffered. The lazy majority punish his unconventionality by dismissing it as funny; not understanding his meaning or refusing to agree with it, they decide that it conceals only another paradox or another attempt to be shocking or sensational. . . . Shaw is possessed of the brightest wit now known to literature. . . . Like any great comic writer . . . , he knows how to destroy error by laughter. . . . Shaw has proved himself the master of most of the devices designed to elicit laughter.

> Carl Van Doren and Mark Van Doren, *American and British Literature Since 1890*, The Century Company, 1925.

4. *He is a writer of marked originality who has developed both satire and drama after his own fashion. He must be regarded as one of the most remarkable contributors to twentieth-century literature.*

> William A. Neilson and Ashley H. Thorndike, *A History of English Literature*, The Macmillan Company, 1927.

5. *He is a reformer and a satirist, and in his plays he does not hesitate to discuss and argue as one might in a tract or a pamphlet. It cannot be said that he excels in constructing plays or creating characters, but no one has written more brilliant and witty dialogue.*

> Neilson and Thorndike, *A History of English Literature*.

6. *His predominant characteristic is a fearless intellectual criticism. . . . He possesses to the highest degree inventive-*

*ness, wit, humour. He knows admirably how to animate
ideas, make them live; and, most of all, how to set them
up one against another; and conduct an intellectual debate.
He has thus invested the most serious thoughts with the
exuberant liveliness of form. . . . Shaw has popularized the
satire of all values by throwing upon it the light of plain,
irresistible comedy. . . .*

> Emile Legouis and Louis Cazamian,
> *A History of English Literature,*
> The Macmillan Company, 1930.

7. *Many of his plays degenerate into endless dialogue,
in which the brilliancy of the verve cannot hide the artificiality of the situation. Profound dramatic life is most often
lacking in his work. The reason is that emotion, the main-
spring of interest, is almost constantly wanting. Bernard
Shaw's characters bear the mark of the conscious will which
has given them birth; few among them stir us with human
sympathy. . . .*

> Legouis and Cazamian, *A History
> of English Literature.*

8. *Why is not Bernard Shaw taken . . . seriously? The
reason is obvious, I think. For while Shaw is always serious,
he is never solemn, and for some obscure reason we are
loath to believe that anyone can mean what he says unless
he pulls a long face while saying it. Wit! That, in one word,
is Shaw's trouble, just as it has been his salvation. . . . The
sugar of his wit is so lavish that it forms a meal by itself;
so audiences who attend his plays find primarily entertain-
ments where they are offered primarily sermons.*

> Maurice Colbourne, *The Real Ber-
> nard Shaw,* Bruce Humphries, Inc.,
> 1931.

9. *Although, as George Jean Nathan remarked, some of
Shaw's plays are as "unemotional as a mushroom," his*

work is rooted in feeling. It reflects a humanitarianism that is as emotional as anything in drama, and there is a noble passion in it. And for all his so-called clowning, his writings are permeated with a dignity that stems equally from an unintimidated mind and a noble spirit. . . . Actually, Shaw has been one of the most humane playwrights of the world.

John Gassner, *Masters of the Drama,* Dover Publications, 1940.

10. *Shaw's own place in literature depends not on the propaganda value of his work, but upon its entertainment value. . . . He gave current English drama a place in the literature of the world. . . . Shaw can be justly charged sometimes with mere fatuity and sometimes with mere facility; but in his best work he has added to the gaiety of thinking and extended the range of rational enjoyment.*

George Sampson, *The Concise Cambridge History of English Literature,* The Dryden Press, 1941.

11. *He fathered a new type, called the play of ideas. For some thirty-odd years he was the most talked about personage in the dramatic world. . . . His forty-odd plays were mostly against the established order and written, as he declared, with intent to make Englishmen drop their outworn beliefs and accept his own, which were invariably of the opposite kind. His motive . . . was to knock all "romantic notions" out of English life and literature—a thing which might be more easily done if romance were not so deeply ingrained in human nature.*

William J. Long, *English Literature,* Ginn and Company, 1945.

12. *It is true that Shaw can be felt in all his plays behind the paper-thin masks of his characters. . . . All of Shaw's*

characters are unbelievable as people, yet not defined as fictions. . . .

> Francis Fergusson, *The Idea of a Theatre*, Doubleday and Company, 1949.

13. *With his prefaces, his speeches, and his plays, he made people think who never thought before. Even when his ideas were not original, he popularized the ideas of others in such a way that the public became aware of them and interested in them for the first time. . . . In fact, it is no exaggeration to say that Shaw's influence, directly or indirectly, may be felt in every branch of human thought. . . . He renovated the British stage. . . . He gave back mind to the drama, awakened the social conscience of his age, made entertainment serve the cause of religion, proved that historical figures are as human and interesting as our own contemporaries, and re-created in the theatre what had long been absent from it: an atmosphere of intelligent gaiety and good fellowship.*

> Hesketh Pearson, *George Bernard Shaw, a Postscript*, Harper and Brothers, 1950.

14. *In giving flaws to his characters, he established their limitations himself. The flaws are generally deliberate creations of his perception of character, his philosophic intelligence, and, above all, his sense of comedy. For it is the business of comedy to note imperfection rather than perfection in man and society, to note imperfection even where merit is also present.*

> John Gassner, *The Theatre in Our Times*, Crown Publishers, 1954.

15. *He was amazingly, continuously, uproariously witty. . . . There was at least one human character that he could depict to the life, and that was his own. In half of his plays, there is one human being who is copied from life*

and appears under different disguises, and that is the infinitely various yet always the same George Bernard Shaw. Apart from that he was not skilled . . . in presenting individual characters; but from his judicious observation of men and women in various classes of English society he formed judgments about types, and those types became the persons of his plays. . . . For the most part, his characters are puppets who speak the words necessary for the part they are taking in the conflict of ideas which make the play; and so much Shavian wit and agreeable absurdity emerge that an intelligent audience cannot fail to be entertained. . . .

R. A. Scott-James, *Fifty Years of English Literature,* Longmans, Green and Company, 1956.

16. *To obtain the greatest effect, he magnifies . . . exaggerates. . . . Contrary to the almost universal belief that Shaw is primarily a satirist rather than a humorist, the truth is that he vigorously disclaims the former label and insists that he is a humorist only intermittently, sporadically. His is not the steady glow of humor, although he is always the humorist when most genial; but we often discern the satirist in the coruscating play of his wit. . . . We may frankly characterize him as a caricaturist. The distinguishing characteristics of the caricaturist are exaggeration and distortion. The distortion is not deviation from, but a heightening of, reality. . . . Shaw is a literary cartoonist. . . .*

Archibald Henderson, *George Bernard Shaw, Man of the Century,* Appleton-Century-Crofts, Inc., 1956.

17. *The characters are much better than many of his critics would have us believe. . . . His limitations are obvious. . . . His dramatic method is far from being subtle. Having learned from his platform experience that earnest people—are always easily amused by broadly comic effects, he never hes-*

itates . . . to introduce some rather rough clowning. . . .
Having once achieved his own comedy of debate, he makes
few experiments in form and technique, is not afraid of wild-
ly improbable situations or of handling his cast as if they
were playing an operetta. Some of the basic situations in his
most successful plays . . . are sheer impudence.

> J. B. Priestley, *Literature and West-*
> *ern Man*, Harper and Brothers,
> 1960.

18. *"Some of the air we breathe now has George Bernard*
Shaw in it, a little mountain oxygen that has somehow
penetrated the fog." This comment of J. B. Priestley's is
perhaps the tribute Shaw himself would most appreciate.
For he wanted above all to clear that air, to make men
think for themselves along new lines in a changing world.
His achievement was that he succeeded and added to the
gaiety of mankind while doing so.

> Audrey Williamson, *Bernard Shaw:*
> *Man and Writer*, Crowell-Collier
> Press, 1963.

19. *He opened the way for a new drama which discussed*
social issues. . . . A number of new writers would have little
or no chance if Shaw had not been a pioneer in showing that
a "problem play" could drive into issues of genuine public
importance.

> Ivor Brown, *Shaw in His Time*,
> Thomas Nelson and Sons, Ltd.,
> 1965.

Certainly the foregoing critical opinions are conflicting, if
not confusing. To bring order out of chaos, you should try
to evaluate the charges in terms of your own estimate of
Shaw's skill in:

a) Characterization

What might be any person's reaction to the rudeness of
Professor Higgins? (p. 26T–M)

Are there fathers who are rather careless about their marital and parental responsibilities? (pp. 34M–39B)

How effectively do Liza's remarks to Colonel Pickering (p. 90T–M) prove that Shaw could probe deeply into his characters' emotions?

Are Professor Higgins's comments on man-woman relationships entirely cold?

b) Stagecraft

Are Shaw's directions for sets and characters too detailed, or are they necessary, as in his description of Professor Higgins (p. 18M–B), to establish the credibility of what is said and done in a particular setting?

Is *Pygmalion* all talk, or is there enough action of a diversified nature to keep an audience interested?

Does each act end on a note of anticipation for the audience? Are we hoping to meet Liza again after Act I, wondering how her speech lessons will turn out (Act II), guessing at the aftermath of her social triumph (Act III), looking forward to her next meeting with Professor Higgins (Act IV)? If we are, is it acceptable to read that Shaw "had no conception of the drama as a literary form"?

c) Style

Hardly anyone disputes Shaw's ability to project wit and wisdom through the dialogue of his characters. Are the lines still funny and pertinent? Millions of people who saw *My Fair Lady* on stage and screen thought so.

20. *The piece did not fail to give us the usual overtone: shrewd, penetrating observations upon society. . . . At the center is the satire directed against the pretensions and conventions of class. The speech of Eliza . . . at first objectionably like her kind and later that of a fine lady, becomes in Shaw's hands a symbol of all the acquired, external touchstones by which people assume superiority and grade social distinction.*

> Burton, *Bernard Shaw, the Man and the Mask.*

21. *Shaw described* Pygmalion *as "intensely and deliberately didactic." That was one of his jokes. . . . Whatever didactic element it contains is so well dramatized that, remaining unstated, it insinuates itself through art. The creation of the artificial duchess suggests that accent, the artificial mark and instrument of caste, is the only difference except wealth between the classes. The inhumanity of Higgins, based upon subtle observation, is thoroughly human. These subtleties, however, do not injure social point.*

> William York Tindall, *Forces in Modern British Literature*, Alfred A. Knopf and Company, 1947.

22. *There was a memorable fury in Shaw. . . . He was the bull in the china-shop of British theatre, and the pieces are still rattling. . . . If we want a British drama on the subject of caste and snobbery . . . we have no further to seek than* Pygmalion. *If we want eloquence on the subject of equality or on some related subject, we need only listen to his Eliza-Galatea telling off her Pygmalion-elocutionist.*

> Gassner, *The Theatre in Our Times.*

23. Pygmalion . . . *presents one side of his Socialist philosophy, the view that the only hope for the future of society and the race is the breaking down of the barriers between the classes. Salvation lies in making it possible for the chauffeur to marry the duchess, the daughter of the dustman to marry the professor of phonetics.*

> Henderson, *George Bernard Shaw, Man of the Century.*

24. *It is not the phonetics which impress those who read or see the play; it is the fine sentiment that the flower girl will behave like a lady when she is treated like one; and that a woman who is only technically a lady is not a lady at all. Expensive education can produce a person who is formally*

at ease in polite company and, at the same time, has the mental and physical outlook of a slut. It was not a course of phonetics which made Eliza display good manners . . . but an inward grace which, like a seed hidden in the soil, germinates only when the conditions are right.

> St. John Ervine, *Bernard Shaw, His Life, Work, and Friends,* William Morrow and Company, 1956.

The main source of controversy about *Pygmalion,* of course, concerns Shaw's ending of the play. Because Shaw publicly scoffed at happy, romantic endings, we can probably understand why he chose to end the play in so indeterminate a fashion. The sketch of Liza's future (pp. 101T–112B) may seem to us as unsatisfactory as it did to many critics. Like the critics, we may wonder whether the epilogue was just another of Shaw's little jokes.

25. *If the complaint be made that he represents too few of the softer and more soothing qualities of human nature, he replies that he thinks those qualities on the whole vicious because they prevent the healthy working of the mind. . . . In* Pygmalion *Professor Higgins, the philologist, takes a young cockney girl into his home to test a theory he has that he can make a lady out of any girl by teaching her to speak like one. He does so to his satisfaction and stops there; Shaw takes pains to prevent him from falling in love with Eliza as any professor would have done in almost any other play.*

> Van Doren and Van Doren, *American and British Literature Since 1890.*

26. *Shaw and all the other Ibsenites were fond of insisting that a defect in the romantic drama was its tendency to end with wedding bells. . . . Many have despised romance because it is unreal; Shaw really hates it because it is a great deal too real. . . . For instance, it is the first duty of a*

man who is in love to make a fool of himself; but Shaw's heroes always seem to flinch from this and attempt, in airy, philosophic revenge, to make a fool of the woman first.

G. K. Chesterton, *George Bernard Shaw*, The Devin-Adair Company, 1950.

27. *I remember being dumbfounded by the conventional strongman and conquered woman ending to the film* Pygmalion. . . . *When I taxed Shaw on the subject, he assured me that he had all along been careful to show that there was not an atom of sex in the Professor and had even written a scene for the film, omitted by the producer, making it perfectly clear that Eliza would marry Freddy.*

Pearson, *George Bernard Shaw, a Postscript.*

28. *The audience's desire to see Higgins at the mercy of Liza does not proceed from the audience's debased and vulgar taste but from the success of Shaw's manipulation of a familiar theme. And it is Shaw himself who has in recent years furnished evidence in support of this contention. Gabriel Pascal's admirable film of* Pygmalion *has a more tenderly romantic conclusion. . . . If Shaw . . . was willing to permit the audience to carry away the impression that Higgins and Liza had been more than reconciled, then one must assume that he changed his mind about the ending of his own play or that his epilogue was something less than serious.*

Milton Crane, "Pygmalion: Bernard Shaw's Dramatic Theory and Practice" in *PMLA,* Volume LXVI, No. 6, December, 1951, Modern Language Association of America.

29. *The epilogue convinces nobody who reads it. . . . The facts of the play cry out against its author. The end of the*

fourth act as well as the end of the fifth act deny the labored account of the flower girl's future and assure all sensible people that she married Henry Higgins.

> Ervine, *Bernard Shaw, His Life, Work, and Friends.*

30. *Shaw balks at making Liza's relations to Higgins those of Cinderella to the Fairy Prince. Shaw permits* Pygmalion *all the trappings of romantic comedy, lets everyone, even Liza, assume that Higgins will marry her, and in the theatre never flatly states that Higgins didn't. Shaw only says that Higgins didn't in the epilogue. . . . But Higgins's lack of susceptibility is what, in the end, gives the play its freshness, and is equally what turns Liza into a hurt and indignant and thus a living woman.*

> Louis Kronenberger in Introduction to *Four Plays by Bernard Shaw,* The Modern Library, 1953.

31. *His refusal to end with a match between Higgins and Eliza was considered mere perversity. Actually Shaw took care to make the ending perfectly ambiguous on the stage and was provoked into writing the long final note for the reader . . . only by the ingenuity of the actors in finding ways to resolve the ambiguity. . . . In a number of ways, the original ambiguity is preferable. . . . The point of the ending is not Eliza's marriage, but her casting loose, her achievement of independence. Almost to the very end Higgins always speaks of having made a duchess of a flower girl, but after her declaration of independence and equality he cries, "By George, Eliza, I said I'd make a woman of you, and I have." (p. 99M)*

> Martin Meisel, *Shaw and the Nineteenth-Century Theatre,* Princeton University Press, 1963.

32. *It was a Shavian ending, refusing to romanticize. . . .*

It is typical of the more romantic media into which the play has been translated in modern times—films and the musical stage—that Eliza ends up with a triumphant although unreformed Higgins.

> Williamson, *Bernard Shaw: Man and Writer.*

If you enjoyed *My Fair Lady* on stage or film, you may be astonished at the following critical evaluation of the musical play.

33. *I think* My Fair Lady *was a hideous desecration of Shaw, and that it could have been so successful is one of the glaring examples of the stupidity of our time.* My Fair Lady *is only one of the debasements of the modern theatre, but it is a special debasement of Shaw. . . .* My Fair Lady *was perpetrated after Shaw's death; at least Oskar Straus's music for* The Chocolate Soldier (*based on Shaw's* Arms and the Man) *was gay and sparkling in the Viennese manner, as the noise made in* My Fair Lady *was not. The distinction between it and* Pygmalion *is not one of degree but of difference:* My Fair Lady *is on the intellectual level of such television programs as* The Beverly Hillbillies. *. . . Yet —who knows? Shaw himself was so impish that, if he were still about, he might well say that he relished* My Fair Lady. *But surely that would be impishness.*

> Harry T. Moore in Preface to *George Bernard Shaw, Creative Artist* by Homer E. Woodbridge.

LIZA. How do you do? [*She sits down on the ottoman gracefully in the place just left vacant by Higgins*].

MRS EYNSFORD HILL [*introducing*] My daughter Clara.

LIZA. How do you do?

CLARA [*impulsively*] How do you do? [*She sits down on the ottoman beside Eliza, devouring her with her eyes*].

FREDDY [*coming to their side of the ottoman*] Ive certainly had the pleasure.

MRS EYNSFORD HILL [*introducing*] My son Freddy.

LIZA. How do you do?

Freddy bows and sits down in the Elizabethan chair, infatuated.

HIGGINS [*suddenly*] By George, yes: it all comes back to me! [*They stare at him*]. Covent Garden! [*Lamentably*] What a damned thing!

MRS HIGGINS. Henry, please! [*He is about to sit on the edge of the table*] Dont sit on my writing-table: youll break it.

HIGGINS [*sulkily*] Sorry.

He goes to the divan, stumbling into the fender and over the fire-irons on his way; extricating himself with muttered imprecations; and finishing his disastrous journey by throwing himself so impatiently on the divan that he almost breaks it. Mrs Higgins looks at him, but controls herself and says nothing.

A long and painful pause ensues.

MRS HIGGINS [*at last, conversationally*] Will it rain, do you think?

LIZA. The shallow depression in the west of these islands is likely to move slowly in an easterly direction. There are no indications of any great change in the barometrical situation.

FREDDY. Ha! ha! how awfully funny!

LIZA. What is wrong with that, young man? I bet I got it right.

FREDDY. Killing!

MRS EYNSFORD HILL. I'm sure I hope it wont turn cold. Theres so much influenza about. It runs right through our whole family regularly every spring.

LIZA [*darkly*] My aunt died of influenza: so they said.

MRS EYNSFORD HILL [*clicks her tongue sympathetically*]!!!

LIZA [*in the same tragic tone*] But it's my belief they done the old woman in.

MRS HIGGINS [*puzzled*] Done her in?

LIZA. Y-e-e-e-es, Lord love you! Why should she die of influenza? She come through diphtheria right enough the year before. I saw her with my own eyes. Fairly blue with it, she was. They all thought she was dead; but my father he kept ladling gin down her throat til she came to so sudden that she bit the bowl off the spoon.

MRS EYNSFORD HILL [*startled*] Dear me!

LIZA [*piling up the indictment*] What call would a woman with that strength in her have to die of influenza? What become of her new straw hat that should have come to me? Somebody pinched it; and what I say is, them as pinched it done her in.

MRS EYNSFORD HILL. What does doing her in mean?

HIGGINS [*hastily*] Oh, thats the new small talk. To do a person in means to kill them.

MRS EYNSFORD HILL [*to Eliza, horrified*] You surely dont believe that your aunt was killed?

LIZA. Do I not! Them she lived with would have killed her for a hat-pin, let alone a hat.

MRS EYNSFORD HILL. But it cant have been right for your father to pour spirits down her throat like that. It might have killed her.

LIZA. Not her. Gin was mother's milk to her. Besides, he'd poured so much down his own throat that he knew the good of it.

MRS EYNSFORD HILL. Do you mean that he drank?

LIZA. Drank! My word! Something chronic.

MRS EYNSFORD HILL. How dreadful for you!

LIZA. Not a bit. It never did him no harm what I could see. But then he did not keep it up regular. [*Cheerfully*] On the burst, as you might say, from time to time. And always more agreeable when he had a drop in. When he was out of work, my mother used to give him fourpence and tell him to go out and not come back until he'd drunk himself cheerful and loving-like. Theres lots of women has to make their husbands drunk to make them fit to live with. [*Now quite at her ease*] You see, it's like this. If a man has a bit of conscience, it always takes him when he's sober; and then it makes him low-spirited. A drop of booze just takes that off and makes him happy. [*To Freddy, who is in convulsions of suppressed laughter*] Here! what are you sniggering at?

FREDDY. The new small talk. You do it so awfully well.

LIZA. If I was doing it proper, what was you laughing at? [*To Higgins*] Have I said anything I oughtnt?

MRS HIGGINS [*interposing*] Not at all, Miss Doolittle.

LIZA. Well, thats a mercy, anyhow. [*Expansively*] What I always say is—

HIGGINS [*rising and looking at his watch*] Ahem!

LIZA [*looking round at him; taking the hint; and rising*] Well: I must go. [*They all rise. Freddy goes to the door*]. So pleased to have met you. Goodbye. [*She shakes hands with Mrs Higgins*].

MRS HIGGINS. Goodbye.

LIZA. Goodbye, Colonel Pickering.

PICKERING. Goodbye, Miss Doolittle. [*They shake hands*].

LIZA [*nodding to the others*] Goodbye, all.

FREDDY [*opening the door for her*] Are you walking across the Park, Miss Doolittle? If so—

LIZA [*with perfectly elegant diction*] Walk! Not bloody likely. [*Sensation*]. I am going in a taxi. [*She goes out*].

Pickering gasps and sits down. Freddy goes out on the balcony to catch another glimpse of Eliza.

MRS EYNSFORD HILL [*suffering from shock*] Well, I really cant get used to the new ways.

CLARA [*throwing herself discontentedly into the Elizabethan chair*] Oh, it's all right, mamma, quite right. People will think we never go anywhere or see anybody if you are so old-fashioned.

MRS EYNSFORD HILL. I daresay I am very old-fashioned; but I do hope you wont begin using that expression, Clara. I have got accustomed to hear you talking about men as rotters, and calling everything filthy and beastly; though I do think it horrible and unlady like. But this last is really too much. Dont you think so, Colonel Pickering?

PICKERING. Dont ask me. Ive been away in India for several years; and manners have changed so much that I sometimes dont know whether I'm at a respectable dinnertable or in a ship's forecastle.

CLARA. It's all a matter of habit. Theres no right or wrong in it. Nobody means anything by it. And it's so quaint, and gives such a smart emphasis to things that are not in themselves very witty. I find the new small talk delightful and quite innocent.

MRS EYNSFORD HILL [*rising*] Well, after that, I think it's time for us to go.

Pickering and Higgins rise.

CLARA [*rising*] Oh yes: we have three at-homes to go to still. Goodbye, Mrs Higgins. Goodbye, Colonel Pickering. Goodbye, Professor Higgins.

HIGGINS [*coming grimly at her from the divan, and accompanying her to the door*] Goodbye. Be sure you try on that small talk at the three at-homes. Dont be nervous about it. Pitch it in strong.

CLARA [*all smiles*] I will. Goodbye. Such nonsense, all this early Victorian prudery!

HIGGINS [*tempting her*] Such damned nonsense!

CLARA. Such bloody nonsense!

MRS EYNSFORD HILL [*convulsively*] Clara!

CLARA. Ha! ha! [*She goes out radiant, conscious of being thoroughly up to date, and is heard descending the stairs in a stream of silvery laughter*].

FREDDY [*to the heavens at large*] Well, I ask you— [*He gives it up, and comes to Mrs Higgins*]. Goodbye.

MRS HIGGINS [*shaking hands*] Goodbye. Would you like to meet Miss Doolittle again?

FREDDY [*eagerly*] Yes, I should, most awfully.

MRS HIGGINS. Well, you know my days.

FREDDY. Yes. Thanks awfully. Goodbye. [*He goes out*].

MRS EYNSFORD HILL. Goodbye, Mr Higgins.

HIGGINS. Goodbye. Goodbye.

MRS EYNSFORD HILL [*to Pickering*] It's no use. I shall never be able to bring myself to use that word.

PICKERING. Dont. It's not compulsory, you know. Youll get on quite well without it.

MRS EYNSFORD HILL. Only, Clara is so down on me if I am not positively reeking with the latest slang. Goodbye.

PICKERING. Goodbye [*They shake hands*].

MRS EYNSFORD HILL [*to Mrs Higgins*] You mustnt mind Clara. [*Pickering, catching from her lowered tone that this is not meant for him to hear, discreetly joins Higgins at the window*]. We're so poor! and she gets so few parties, poor child! She doesnt quite know. [*Mrs Higgins, seeing that her eyes are moist, takes her hand sympathetically and goes with her to the door*]. But the boy is nice. Dont you think so?

MRS HIGGINS. Oh, quite nice. I shall always be delighted to see him.

MRS EYNSFORD HILL. Thank you, dear. Goodbye. [*She goes out*].

HIGGINS [*eagerly*] Well? Is Eliza presentable [*he swoops on his mother and drags her to the ottoman, where she sits down in Eliza's place with her son on her left*]?

Pickering returns to his chair on her right.

MRS HIGGINS. You silly boy, of course she's not presentable. She's a triumph of your art and of her dressmaker's; but if you suppose for a moment that she doesn't give herself away in every sentence she utters, you must be perfectly cracked about her.

PICKERING. But dont you think something might be done? I mean something to eliminate the sanguinary element from her conversation.

MRS HIGGINS. Not as long as she is in Henry's hands.

HIGGINS [*aggrieved*] Do you mean that my language is improper?

MRS HIGGINS. No dearest: it would be quite proper—say on a canal barge; but it would not be proper for her at a garden party.

HIGGINS [*deeply injured*] Well I must say—

PICKERING [*interrupting him*] Come, Higgins: you must learn to know yourself. I havent heard such language as yours since we used to review the volunteers in Hyde Park twenty years ago.

HIGGINS [*sulkily*] Oh, well, if you say so, I suppose I dont always talk like a bishop.

MRS HIGGINS [*quieting Henry with a touch*] Colonel Pickering: will you tell me what is the exact state of things in Wimpole Street?

PICKERING [*cheerfully: as if this completely changed the subject*] Well, I have come to live there with Henry. We work together at my Indian Dialects; and we think it more convenient—

MRS HIGGINS. Quite so. I know all about that: it's an excellent arrangement. But where does this girl live?

HIGGINS. With us, of course. Where should she live?

MRS HIGGINS. But on what terms? Is she a servant? If not, what is she?

PICKERING [*slowly*] I think I know what you mean, Mrs Higgins.

HIGGINS. Well, dash me if *I* do! Ive had to work at the girl every day for months to get her to her present pitch. Besides, she's useful. She knows where my things are, and remembers my appointments and so forth.

MRS HIGGINS. How does your housekeeper get on with her?

HIGGINS. Mrs Pearce? Oh, she's jolly glad to get so much taken off her hands; for before Eliza came, she used to have to find things and remind me of my appointments. But she's got some silly bee in her bonnet about Eliza. She keeps saying "You dont think, sir": doesnt she, Pick?

PICKERING. Yes: thats the formula. "You dont think, sir." Thats the end of every conversation about Eliza.

HIGGINS. As if I ever stop thinking about the girl and her confounded vowels and consonants. I'm worn out, thinking about her, and watching her lips and her teeth and her tongue, not to mention her soul, which is the quaintest of the lot.

MRS HIGGINS. You certainly are a pretty pair of babies, playing with your live doll.

HIGGINS. Playing! The hardest job I ever tackled: make no mistake about that, mother. But you have no idea how frightfully interesting it is to take a human being and change her into a quite different human being by creating a new speech for her. It's filling up the deepest gulf that separates class from class and soul from soul.

PICKERING [*drawing his chair closer to Mrs Higgins and bending over to her eagerly*] Yes: it's enormously interesting. I assure you, Mrs Higgins, we take Eliza very seriously. Every week—every day almost—there is some new change. [*Closer again*] We keep records of every stage—dozens of gramophone disks and photographs—

HIGGINS [*assailing her at the other ear*] Yes, by George: it's the most absorbing experiment I ever tackled. She regularly fills our lives up: doesnt she, Pick?

PICKERING. We're always talking Eliza.

HIGGINS. Teaching Eliza.

PICKERING. Dressing Eliza.

MRS HIGGINS. What!

HIGGINS. Inventing new Elizas.

HIGGINS.	*[speaking together]*	You know, she has the most extraordinary quickness of ear:
PICKERING.		I assure you, my dear Mrs Higgins, that girl
HIGGINS.		just like a parrot. Ive tried her with every
PICKERING.		is a genius. She can play the piano quite beautifully.
HIGGINS.		possible sort of sound that a human being can make—
PICKERING.		We have taken her to classical concerts and to music
HIGGINS.		Continental dialects, African dialects, Hottentot
PICKERING.		halls; and it's all the same to her: she plays everything
HIGGINS.		clicks, things it took me years to get hold of; and
PICKERING.		she hears right off when she comes home, whether it's
HIGGINS.		she picks them up like a shot, right away, as if she had
PICKERING.		Beethoven and Brahms or Lehar and Lionel Monckton;
HIGGINS.		been at it all her life.
PICKERING.		though six months ago, she'd never as much as touched a piano—

MRS HIGGINS [*putting her fingers in her ears, as they are by this time shouting one another down with an intolerable noise*] Sh-sh-sh—sh! [*They stop*].

PICKERING. I beg your pardon. [*He draws his chair back apologetically*].

HIGGINS. Sorry. When Pickering starts shouting nobody can get a word in edgeways.

MRS HIGGINS. Be quiet, Henry. Colonel Pickering: dont you realize that when Eliza walked in Wimpole Street, something walked in with her?

PICKERING. Her father did. But Henry soon got rid of him.

MRS HIGGINS. It would have been more to the point if her mother had. But as her mother didnt something else did.

PICKERING. But what?

MRS HIGGINS [*unconsciously dating herself by the word*] A problem.

PICKERING. Oh, I see. The problem of how to pass her off as a lady.

HIGGINS. I'll solve that problem. Ive half solved it already.

MRS HIGGINS. No, you two infinitely stupid male creatures: the problem of what is to be done with her afterwards.

HIGGINS. I dont see anything in that. She can go her own way, with all the advantages I have given her.

MRS HIGGINS. The advantages of that poor woman who was here just now! The manners and habits that disqualify a fine lady from earning her own living without giving her a fine lady's income! Is that what you mean?

PICKERING [*indulgently, being rather bored*] Oh, that will be all right, Mrs Higgins. [*He rises to go*].

HIGGINS [*rising also*] We'll find her some light employment.

PICKERING. She's happy enough. Dont you worry about her. Goodbye. [*He shakes hands as if he were consoling a frightened child, and makes for the door*].

HIGGINS. Anyhow, theres no good bothering now. The thing's done. Goodbye, mother. [*He kisses her, and follows Pickering*].

PICKERING [*turning for a final consolation*] There are plenty of openings. We'll do whats right. Goodbye.

HIGGINS [*to Pickering as they go out together*] Lets take her to the Shakespear exhibition at Earls Court.

PICKERING. Yes: lets. Her remarks will be delicious.

HIGGINS. She'll mimic all the people for us when we get home.

PICKERING. Ripping. [*Both are heard laughing as they go downstairs*].

MRS HIGGINS [*rising with an impatient bounce, and returns to her work at the writing-table. She sweeps a litter of disarranged papers out of the way; snatches a sheet of paper from her stationery case; and tries resolutely to write. At the third time she gives it up; flings down her pen; grips the table angrily and exclaims*] Oh, men! men!! men!!!

✺   ✺   ✺   ✺   ✺   ✺

Clearly Eliza will not pass as a duchess yet; and Higgins's bet remains unwon. But the six months are not yet exhausted and just in time Eliza does actually pass as a princess. For a glimpse of how she did it imagine an Embassy in London one summer evening after dark. The hall door has an awning and a carpet across the sidewalk to the kerb, because a grand reception is in progress. A small crowd is lined up to see the guests arrive.

A Rolls-Royce car drives up. Pickering in evening dress, with medals and orders, alights, and hands out Eliza, in opera cloak, evening dress, diamonds, fan, flowers and all accessories. Higgins follows. The car drives off; and the three go up the steps and into the house, the door opening for them as they approach.

Inside the house they find themselves in a spacious hall from which the grand staircase rises. On the left are the arrangements for the gentlemen's cloaks. The male guests are depositing their hats and wraps there.

On the right is a door leading to the ladies' cloakroom. Ladies are going in cloaked and coming out in splendor. Pickering whispers to Eliza and points out the ladies' room. She goes into it. Higgins and Pickering take off their overcoats and take tickets for them from the attendant.

One of the guests, occupied in the same way, has his back turned. Having taken his ticket, he turns round and reveals himself as an important looking young man with an astonishingly hairy face. He has an enormous moustache, flowing out into luxuriant whiskers. Waves of hair cluster on his brow. His hair is cropped closely at the back, and glows with oil. Otherwise he is very smart. He wears several worthless orders. He is evidently a foreigner, guessable as a whiskered Pandour from Hungary; but in spite of the ferocity of his moustache he is amiable and genially voluble.

Recognizing Higgins, he flings his arms wide apart and approaches him enthusiastically.

WHISKERS. Maestro, maestro [*he embraces Higgins and kisses him on both cheeks*]. You remember me?

HIGGINS. No I dont. Who the devil are you?

WHISKERS. I am your pupil: your first pupil, your best and greatest pupil. I am little Nepommuck, the marvellous boy. I have made your name famous throughout Europe. You teach me phonetic. You cannot forget ME.

HIGGINS. Why dont you shave?

NEPOMMUCK. I have not your imposing appearance, your

chin, your brow. Nobody notice me when I shave. Now I am famous: they call me Hairy Faced Dick.

HIGGINS. And what are you doing here among all these swells?

NEPOMMUCK. I am interpreter. I speak 32 languages. I am indispensable at these international parties. You are great cockney specialist: you place a man anywhere in London the moment he open his mouth. I place any man in Europe.

A footman hurries down the grand staircase and comes to Nepommuck.

FOOTMAN. You are wanted upstairs. Her Excellency cannot understand the Greek gentleman.

NEPOMMUCK. Thank you, yes, immediately.

The footman goes and is lost in the crowd.

NEPOMMUCK [*to Higgins*] This Greek diplomatist pretends he cannot speak nor understand English. He cannot deceive me. He is the son of a Clerkenwell watchmaker. He speaks English so villainously that he dare not utter a word of it without betraying his origin. I help him to pretend; but I make him pay through the nose. I make them all pay. Ha ha! [*He hurries upstairs*].

PICKERING. Is this fellow really an expert? Can he find out Eliza and blackmail her?

HIGGINS. We shall see. If he finds her out I lose my bet.

Eliza comes from the cloakroom and joins them.

PICKERING. Well, Eliza, now for it. Are you ready?

LIZA. Are you nervous, Colonel?

PICKERING. Frightfully. I feel exactly as I felt before my first battle. It's the first time that frightens.

LIZA. It is not the first time for me, Colonel. I have done this fifty times—hundreds of times—in my little piggery in Angel Court in my day-dreams. I am in a dream now. Promise me not to let Professor Higgins wake me; for if he does I shall forget everything and talk as I used to in Drury Lane.

PICKERING. Not a word, Higgins. [*To Eliza*] Now, ready?

LIZA. Ready.

PICKERING. Go.

They mount the stairs, Higgins last. Pickering whispers to the footman on the first landing.

FIRST LANDING FOOTMAN. Miss Doolittle, Colonel Pickering, Professor Higgins.

SECOND LANDING FOOTMAN. Miss Doolittle, Colonel Pickering, Professor Higgins.

At the top of the staircase the Ambassador and his wife, with Nepommuck at her elbow, are receiving.

HOSTESS [*taking Eliza's hand*] How d'ye do?

HOST [*same play*] How d'ye do? How d'ye do, Pickering?

LIZA [*with a beautiful gravity that awes her hostess*] How do you do? [*She passes on to the drawingroom*].

HOSTESS. Is that your adopted daughter, Colonel Pickering? She will make a sensation.

PICKERING. Most kind of you to invite her for me. [*He passes on*].

HOSTESS [*to Nepommuck*] Find out all about her.

NEPOMMUCK [*bowing*] Excellency—[*he goes into the crowd*].

HOST. How d'ye do, Higgins? You have a rival here tonight. He introduced himself as your pupil. Is he any good?

HIGGINS. He can learn a language in a fortnight—knows dozens of them. A sure mark of a fool. As a phonetician, no good whatever.

HOSTESS. How d'ye do, Professor?

HIGGINS. How do you do? Fearful bore for you this sort of thing. Forgive my part in it. [*He passes on*].

In the drawingroom and its suite of salons the reception is in full swing. Eliza passes through. She is so intent on her ordeal that she walks like a somnambulist in a desert instead of a débutante in a fashionable crowd. They stop talking to look at her, admiring her dress, her jewels, and her strangely attractive self. Some of the younger ones at the back stand on their chairs to see.

The Host and Hostess come in from the staircase and mingle with their guests. Higgins, gloomy and contemptuous of the whole business, comes into the group where they are chatting.

HOSTESS. Ah, here is Professor Higgins: he will tell us. Tell us all about the wonderful young lady, Professor.

HIGGINS [*almost morosely*] What wonderful young lady?

HOSTESS. You know very well. They tell me there has been nothing like her in London since people stood on their chairs to look at Mrs Langtry.

Nepommuck joins the group, full of news.

HOSTESS. Ah, here you are at last, Nepommuck. Have you found out all about the Doolittle lady?

NEPOMMUCK. I have found out all about her. She is a fraud.

HOSTESS. A fraud! Oh no.

NEPOMMUCK. YES, yes. She cannot deceive me. Her name cannot be Doolittle.

HIGGINS. Why?

NEPOMMUCK. Because Doolittle is an English name. And she is not English.

HOSTESS. Oh, nonsense! She speaks English perfectly.

NEPOMMUCK. Too perfectly. Can you shew me any English woman who speaks English as it should be spoken? Only foreigners who have been taught to speak it speak it well.

HOSTESS. Certainly she terrified me by the way she said How d'ye do. I had a schoolmistress who talked like that; and I was mortally afraid of her. But if she is not English what is she?

NEPOMMUCK. Hungarian.

ALL THE REST. Hungarian!

NEPOMMUCK. Hungarian. And of royal blood. I am Hungarian. My blood is royal.

HIGGINS. Did you speak to her in Hungarian?

NEPOMMUCK. I did. She was very clever. She said "Please speak to me in English: I do not understand French." French! She pretend not to know the difference between Hungarian and French. Impossible: she knows both.

HIGGINS. And the blood royal? How did you find that out?

NEPOMMUCK. Instinct, maestro, instinct. Only the Magyar races can produce that air of the divine right, those resolute eyes. She is a princess.

HOST. What do you say, Professor?

HIGGINS. I say an ordinary London girl out of the gutter and taught to speak by an expert. I place her in Drury Lane.

NEPOMMUCK. Ha ha ha! Oh, maestro, maestro, you are mad on the subject of cockney dialects. The London gutter is the whole world for you.

HIGGINS [*to the Hostess*] What does your Excellency say?

HOSTESS. Oh, of course I agree with Nepommuck. She must be a princess at least.

HOST. Not necessarily legitimate, of course. Morganatic perhaps. But that is undoubtedly her class.

HIGGINS. I stick to my opinion.

HOSTESS. Oh, you are incorrigible.

The group breaks up, leaving Higgins isolated. Pickering joins him.

PICKERING. Where is Eliza? We must keep an eye on her.

Eliza joins them.

LIZA. I dont think I can bear much more. The people all stare so at me. An old lady has just told me that I speak exactly like Queen Victoria. I am sorry if I have lost your bet. I have done my best; but nothing can make me the same as these people.

PICKERING. You have not lost it, my dear. You have won it ten times over.

HIGGINS. Let us get out of this. I have had enough of chattering to these fools.

PICKERING. Eliza is tired; and I am hungry. Let us clear out and have supper somewhere.

PYGMALION

— • • —

ACT IV

ACT IV

The Wimpole Street laboratory. Midnight. Nobody in the room. The clock on the mantelpiece strikes twelve. The fire is not alight: it is a summer night.

Presently Higgins and Pickering are heard on the stairs.

HIGGINS [*calling down to Pickering*] I say, Pick: lock up, will you? I shant be going out again.

PICKERING. Right. Can Mrs Pearce go to bed? We dont want anything more, do we?

HIGGINS. Lord, no!

Eliza opens the door and is seen on the lighted landing in all the finery in which she has just won Higgins's bet for him. She comes to the hearth, and switches on the electric lights there. She is tired: her pallor contrasts strongly with her dark eyes and hair; and her expression is almost tragic. She takes off her cloak; puts her fan and gloves on the piano; and sits down on the bench, brooding and silent. Higgins, in evening dress, with overcoat and hat, comes in, carrying a smoking jacket which he has picked up downstairs. He takes off the hat and overcoat; throws them carelessly on the newspaper stand; disposes of his coat in the same way; puts on the smoking jacket; and throws himself wearily into the easy-chair at the hearth. Pickering, similarly attired, comes in. He also takes off his hat and overcoat, and is about to throw them on Higgins's when he hesitates.

PICKERING. I say: Mrs Pearce will row if we leave these things lying about in the drawing room.

HIGGINS. Oh, chuck them over the bannisters into the hall. She'll find them there in the morning and put them away all right. She'll think we were drunk.

PICKERING. We are, slightly. Are there any letters?

HIGGINS. I didnt look. [*Pickering takes the overcoats and hats and goes downstairs. Higgins begins half singing half yawning an air from La Fanciulla del Golden West. Suddenly he stops and exclaims*] I wonder where the devil my slippers are!

Eliza looks at him darkly; then rises suddenly and leaves the room.

Higgins yawns again, and resumes his song.

Pickering returns, with the contents of the letter-box in his hand.

PICKERING. Only circulars, and this coroneted billet-doux for you. [*He throws the circulars into the fender, and posts himself on the hearth-rug, with his back to the grate*].

HIGGINS [*glancing at the billet-doux*] Money-lender. [*He throws the letter after the circulars.*]

Eliza returns with a pair of large down-at-heel slippers. She places them on the carpet before Higgins, and sits as before without a word.

HIGGINS [*yawning again*] Oh Lord! What an evening! What a crew! What a silly tomfoolery! [*He raises his shoe to unlace it, and catches sight of the slippers. He stops unlacing and looks at them as if they had appeared there of their own accord*]. Oh! theyre there, are they?

PICKERING [*stretching himself*] Well, I feel a bit tired. It's been a long day. The garden party, a dinner party, and the reception! Rather too much of a good thing. But youve won your bet, Higgins. Eliza did the trick, and something to spare, eh?

HIGGINS [*fervently*] Thank God it's over!

Eliza flinches violently; but they take no notice of her; and she recovers herself and sits stonily as before.

PICKERING. Were you nervous at the garden party? *I* was. Eliza didnt seem a bit nervous.

HIGGINS. Oh, she wasnt nervous. I knew she'd be all right. No: it's the strain of putting the job through all these months that has told on me. It was interesting enough at first, while we were at the phonetics; but after that I got deadly sick of it. If I hadnt backed myself to do it I should have chucked the whole thing up two months ago. It was a silly notion: the whole thing has been a bore.

PICKERING. Oh come! the garden party was frightfully exciting. My heart began beating like anything.

HIGGINS. Yes, for the first three minutes. But when I saw we were going to win hands down, I felt like a bear in a cage, hanging about doing nothing. The dinner was worse: sitting gorging there for over an hour, with nobody but a damned fool of a fashionable woman to talk to! I tell you, Pickering, never again for me. No more artificial duchesses. The whole thing has been simple purgatory.

PICKERING. Youve never been broken in properly to the social routine. [*Strolling over to the piano*] I rather enjoy dipping into it occasionally myself: it makes me feel young again. Anyhow, it was a great success: an immense success. I was quite frightened once or twice because Eliza was doing it so well. You see, lots of the real people cant do it at all: theyre such fools that they think style comes by nature to people in their positions; and so they never learn. Theres always something professional about doing a thing superlatively well.

HIGGINS. Yes: thats what drives me mad: the silly people dont know their own silly business. [*Rising*] However, it's over and done with; and now I can go to bed at last without dreading tomorrow.

Eliza's beauty becomes murderous.

PICKERING. I think I shall turn in too. Still, it's been a great occasion: a triumph for you. Goodnight. [*He goes*].

HIGGINS [*following him*] Goodnight. [*Over his shoulder, at the door*] Put out the lights, Eliza; and tell Mrs Pearce not to make coffee for me in the morning: I'll take tea. [*He goes out*].

Eliza tries to control herself and feel indifferent as she rises and walks across to the hearth to switch off the lights. By the time she gets there she is on the point of screaming. She sits down in Higgins's chair and holds on hard to the arms. Finally she gives way and flings herself furiously on the floor, raging.

HIGGINS [*in despairing wrath outside*] What the devil have I done with my slippers? [*He appears at the door*].

LIZA [*snatching up the slippers, and hurling them at him one after the other with all her force*] There are your slippers. And there. Take your slippers; and may you never have a day's luck with them!

HIGGINS [*astounded*] What on earth—! [*He comes to her*]. Whats the matter? Get up. [*He pulls her up*]. Anything wrong?

LIZA [*breathless*] Nothing wrong—with you. Ive won your bet for you, havnt I? Thats enough for you. *I* dont matter, I suppose.

HIGGINS. You won my bet! You! Presumptuous insect! *I* won it. What did you throw those slippers at me for?

LIZA. Because I wanted to smash your face. I'd like to kill you, you selfish brute. Why didnt you leave me where you picked me out of—in the gutter? You thank God it's all over, and that now you can throw me back again there, do you? [*She crisps her fingers frantically*].

HIGGINS [*looking at her in cool wonder*] The creature is nervous, after all.

LIZA [*gives a suffocated scream of fury, and instinctively darts her nails at his face*]!!

HIGGINS [*catching her wrists*] Ah! would you? Claws in, you cat. How dare you shew your temper to me? Sit down and be quiet. [*He throws her roughly into the easy-chair*].

LIZA [*crushed by superior strength and weight*] Whats to become of me? Whats to become of me?

HIGGINS. How the devil do I know whats to become of you? What does it matter what becomes of you?

LIZA. You dont care. I know you dont care. You wouldnt care if I was dead. I'm nothing to you—not so much as them slippers.

HIGGINS [*thundering*] Those slippers.

LIZA [*with bitter submission*] Those slippers. I didnt think it made any difference now.

A pause. Eliza hopeless and crushed. Higgins a little uneasy.

HIGGINS [*in his loftiest manner*] Why have you begun going on like this? May I ask whether you complain of your treatment here?

LIZA. No.

HIGGINS. Has anybody behaved badly to you? Colonel Pickering? Mrs Pearce? Any of the servants?

LIZA. No.

HIGGINS. I presume you dont pretend that *I* have treated you badly?

LIZA. No.

HIGGINS. I am glad to hear it. [*He moderates his tone*]. Perhaps youre tired after the strain of the day. Will you have a glass of champagne? [*He moves towards the door*].

LIZA. No. [*Recollecting her manners*] Thank you.

HIGGINS [*good-humored again*] This has been coming on you for some days. I suppose it was natural for you to be anxious about the garden party. But thats all over now. [*He pats her kindly on the shoulder. She writhes*]. Theres nothing more to worry about.

LIZA. No. Nothing more for you to worry about. [*She suddenly rises and gets away from him by going to the piano bench, where she sits and hides her face*]. Oh God! I wish I was dead.

HIGGINS [*staring after her in sincere surprise*] Why? In heaven's name, why? [*Reasonably, going to her*] Listen to me, Eliza. All this irritation is purely subjective.

LIZA. I dont understand. I'm too ignorant.

HIGGINS. It's only imagination. Low spirits and nothing else. Nobody's hurting you. Nothing's wrong. You go to bed like a good girl and sleep it off. Have a little cry and say your prayers: that will make you comfortable.

LIZA. I heard your prayers. "Thank God it's all over!"

HIGGINS [*impatiently*] Well, dont you thank God it's all over? Now you are free and can do what you like.

LIZA [*pulling herself together in desperation*] What am I fit for? What have you left me fit for? Where am I to go? What am I to do? Whats to become of me?

HIGGINS [*enlightened, but not at all impressed*] Oh, thats whats worrying you, is it? [*He thrusts his hands into his pockets, and walks about in his usual manner, rattling the contents of his pockets, as if condescending to a trivial subject out of pure kindness*]. I shouldnt bother about it if I were you. I should imagine you wont have much difficulty in settling yourself somewhere or other, though I hadnt quite realized that you were going away. [*She looks quickly at him: he does not look at her, but examines the dessert stand on the piano and decides that he will eat an apple*]. You might marry, you know. [*He bites a large piece out of the apple and munches it noisily*]. You see, Eliza, all men are not confirmed old bachelors like me and the Colonel. Most men are the marrying sort (poor devils!); and youre not bad-looking: it's quite a pleasure to look at you sometimes—not now, of course, because youre crying and looking as ugly as the very devil; but when youre all right and quite yourself, youre what I should call attractive. That is, to the people in the marrying line, you understand. You go to bed and have a good nice rest; and then get up and look at yourself in the glass; and you wont feel so cheap.

Eliza again looks at him, speechless, and does not stir.

The look is quite lost on him: he eats his apple with a dreamy expression of happiness, as it is quite a good one.

HIGGINS [*a genial afterthought occurring to him*] I daresay my mother could find some chap or other who would do very well.

LIZA. We were above that at the corner of Tottenham Court Road.

HIGGINS [*waking up*] What do you mean?

LIZA. I sold flowers. I didnt sell myself. Now youve made a lady of me I'm not fit to sell anything else. I wish youd left me where you found me.

HIGGINS [*slinging the core of the apple decisively into the grate*] Tosh, Eliza. Dont you insult human relations by dragging all this cant about buying and selling into it. You neednt marry the fellow if you don't like him.

LIZA. What else am I to do?

HIGGINS. Oh, lots of things. What about your old idea of a florist's shop? Pickering could set you up in one: he has lots of money. [*Chuckling*] He'll have to pay for all those togs you have been wearing today; and that, with the hire of the jewellery, will make a big hole in two hundred pounds. Why, six months ago you would have thought it the millennium to have a flower shop of your own. Come! youll be all right. I must clear off to bed: I'm devilish sleepy. By the way. I came down for something: I forgot what it was.

LIZA. Your slippers.

HIGGINS. Oh yes, of course. You shied them at me. [*He picks them up, and is going out when she rises and speaks to him*].

LIZA. Before you go, sir—

HIGGINS [*dropping the slippers in his surprise at her calling him Sir*] Eh?

The light goes out.

FREDDY. Goodnight, darling, darling, darling.

Eliza comes out, giving the door a considerable bang behind her.

LIZA. Whatever are you doing here?

FREDDY. Nothing. I spend most of my nights here. It's the only place where I'm happy. Dont laugh at me, Miss Doolittle.

LIZA. Dont you call me Miss Doolittle, do you hear? Liza's good enough for me. [*She breaks down and grabs him by the shoulders*] Freddy: you dont think I'm a heartless guttersnipe, do you?

FREDDY. Oh no, no, darling: how can you imagine such a thing? You are the loveliest, dearest—

He loses all self-control and smothers her with kisses. She, hungry for comfort, responds. They stand there in one another's arms.

An elderly police constable arrives.

CONSTABLE [*scandalized*] Now then! Now then!! Now then!!!

They release one another hastily.

FREDDY. Sorry, constable. Weve only just become engaged.

They run away.

The constable shakes his head, reflecting on his own courtship and on the vanity of human hopes. He moves off in the opposite direction with slow professional steps.

The flight of the lovers takes them to Cavendish Square. There they halt to consider their next move.

LIZA [*out of breath*] He didnt half give me a fright, that copper. But you answered him proper.

FREDDY. I hope I havnt taken you out of your way. Where were you going?

LIZA. To the river.

FREDDY. What for?

LIZA. To make a hole in it.

FREDDY [*horrified*] Eliza, darling. What do you mean? Whats the matter?

LIZA. Never mind. It doesnt matter now. Theres nobody in the world now but you and me, is there?

FREDDY. Not a soul.

They indulge in another embrace, and are again surprised by a much younger constable.

SECOND CONSTABLE. Now then, you two! Whats this? Where do you think you are? Move along here, double quick.

FREDDY. As you say, sir, double quick.

They run away again, and are in Hanover Square before they stop for another conference.

FREDDY. I had no idea the police were so devilishly prudish.

LIZA. It's their business to hunt girls off the streets.

FREDDY. We must go somewhere. We cant wander about the streets all night.

LIZA. Cant we? I think it'd be lovely to wander about for ever.

FREDDY. Oh, darling.

They embrace again, oblivious of the arrival of a crawling taxi. It stops.

TAXIMAN. Can I drive you and the lady anywhere, sir?

They start asunder.

LIZA. Oh, Freddy, a taxi. The very thing.

FREDDY. But, damn it, Ive no money.

LIZA. I have plenty. The Colonel thinks you should never go out without ten pounds in your pocket. Listen. We'll drive about all night; and in the morning I'll call on old Mrs Higgins and ask her what I ought to do. I'll tell you all about it in the cab. And the police wont touch us there.

FREDDY. Righto! Ripping. [*To the Taximan*] Wimbledon Common. [*They drive off*].

PYGMALION

—••—

ACT V

ACT V

Mrs Higgins's drawing room. She is at her writing-table as before. The parlormaid comes in.

THE PARLORMAID [*at the door*] Mr Henry, maam, is downstairs with Colonel Pickering.

MRS HIGGINS. Well, shew them up.

THE PARLORMAID. Theyre using the telephone, maam. Telephoning to the police, I think.

MRS HIGGINS. What!

THE PARLORMAID [*coming further in and lowering her voice*] Mr Henry is in a state, maam. I thought I'd better tell you.

MRS HIGGINS. If you had told me that Mr Henry was not in a state it would have been more surprising. Tell them to come up when theyve finished with the police. I suppose he's lost something.

THE PARLORMAID. Yes, maam [*going*].

MRS HIGGINS. Go upstairs and tell Miss Doolittle that Mr Henry and the Colonel are here. Ask her not to come down til I send for her.

THE PARLORMAID. Yes, maam.

Higgins bursts in. He is, as the parlormaid has said, in a state.

HIGGINS. Look here, mother: heres a confounded thing!

MRS HIGGINS. Yes, dear. Good morning. [*He checks his impatience and kisses her, whilst the parlormaid goes out*]. What is it?

HIGGINS. Eliza's bolted.

MRS HIGGINS [*calmly continuing her writing*] You must have frightened her.

HIGGINS. Frightened her! nonsense! She was left last night, as usual, to turn out the lights and all that; and instead of going to bed she changed her clothes and went right off: her bed wasnt slept in. She came in a cab for her things before seven this morning; and that fool Mrs Pearce let her have them without telling me a word about it. What am I to do?

MRS HIGGINS. Do without, I'm afraid, Henry. The girl has a perfect right to leave if she chooses.

HIGGINS [*wandering distractedly across the room*] But I cant find anything. I dont know what appointments Ive got. I'm—[*Pickering comes in. Mrs Higgins puts down her pen and turns away from the writing-table*].

PICKERING [*shaking hands*] Good morning, Mrs Higgins. Has Henry told you? [*He sits down on the ottoman*].

HIGGINS. What does that ass of an inspector say? Have you offered a reward?

MRS HIGGINS [*rising in indignant amazement*] You dont mean to say you have set the police after Eliza.

HIGGINS. Of course. What are the police for? What else could we do? [*He sits in the Elizabethan chair*].

PICKERING. The inspector made a lot of difficulties. I really think he suspected us of some improper purpose.

MRS HIGGINS. Well, of course he did. What right have you to go to the police and give the girl's name as if she were a thief, or a lost umbrella, or something? Really! [*She sits down again, deeply vexed*].

HIGGINS. But we want to find her.

PICKERING. We cant let her go like this, you know, Mrs Higgins. What were we to do?

MRS HIGGINS. You have no more sense, either of you, than two children. Why—

The parlormaid comes in and breaks off the conversation.

THE PARLORMAID. Mr Henry: a gentleman wants to see you very particular. He's been sent on from Wimpole Street.

HIGGINS. Oh, bother! I cant see anyone now. Who is it?

THE PARLORMAID. A Mr Doolittle, sir.

PICKERING. Doolittle! Do you mean the dustman?

THE PARLORMAID. Dustman! Oh no, sir: a gentleman.

HIGGINS [*springing up excitedly*] By George, Pick, it's some relative of hers that she's gone to. Somebody we know nothing about. [*To the parlormaid*] Send him up, quick.

THE PARLORMAID. Yes, sir. [*She goes*].

HIGGINS [*eagerly, going to his mother*] Genteel relatives! now we shall hear something. [*He sits down in the Chippendale chair*].

MRS HIGGINS. Do you know any of her people?

PICKERING. Only her father: the fellow we told you about.

THE PARLORMAID [*announcing*] Mr Doolittle. [*She withdraws*].

Doolittle enters. He is resplendently dressed as for a fashionable wedding, and might, in fact, be the bridegroom. A flower in his buttonhole, a dazzling silk hat, and patent leather shoes complete the effect. He is too concerned with the business he has come on to notice Mrs Higgins. He walks straight to Higgins, and accosts him with vehement reproach.

DOOLITTLE [*indicating his own person*] See here! Do you see this? You done this.

HIGGINS. Done what, man?

DOOLITTLE. This, I tell you. Look at it. Look at this hat. Look at this coat.

PICKERING. Has Eliza been buying you clothes?

DOOLITTLE. Eliza! not she. Why would she buy me clothes?

MRS HIGGINS. Good morning, Mr Doolittle. Wont you sit down?

DOOLITTLE [*taken aback as he becomes conscious that he has forgotten his hostess*] Asking your pardon, maam. [*He approaches her and shakes her proffered hand*]. Thank you. [*He sits down on the ottoman, on Pickering's right*]. I am that full of what has happened to me that I cant think of anything else.

HIGGINS. What the dickens has happened to you?

DOOLITTLE. I shouldnt mind if it had only happened to me: anything might happen to anybody and nobody to blame but Providence, as you might say. But this is something that you done to me: yes, you, Enry Iggins.

HIGGINS. Have you found Eliza?

DOOLITTLE. Have you lost her?

HIGGINS. Yes.

DOOLITTLE. You have all the luck, you have. I aint found

her; but she'll find me quick enough now after what you done to me.

MRS HIGGINS. But what has my son done to you, Mr Doolittle?

DOOLITTLE. Done to me! Ruined me. Destroyed my happiness. Tied me up and delivered me into the hands of middle class morality.

HIGGINS [*rising intolerantly and standing over Doolittle*] Youre raving. Youre drunk. Youre mad. I gave you five pounds. After that I had two conversations with you, at half-a-crown an hour. Ive never seen you since.

DOOLITTLE. Oh! Drunk am I? Mad am I? Tell me this. Did you or did you not write a letter to an old blighter in America that was giving five millions to found Moral Reform Societies all over the world, and that wanted you to invent a universal language for him?

HIGGINS. What! Ezra D. Wannafeller! He's dead. [*He sits down again carelessly*].

DOOLITTLE. Yes: he's dead; and I'm done for. Now did you or did you not write a letter to him to say that the most original moralist at present in England, to the best of your knowledge, was Alfred Doolittle, a common dustman?

HIGGINS. Oh, after your first visit I remember making some silly joke of the kind.

DOOLITTLE. Ah! you may well call it a silly joke. It put the lid on me right enough. Just give him the chance he wanted to shew that Americans is not like us: that they reckonize and respect merit in every class of life, however humble. Them words is in his blooming will, in which, Henry Higgins, thanks to your silly joking, he leaves me a share in his Pre-digested Cheese Trust worth four thousand a year on condition that I lecture for his Wannafeller Moral Reform World League as often as they ask me up to six times a year.

HIGGINS. The devil he does! Whew! [*Brightening suddenly*] What a lark!

PICKERING. A safe thing for you, Doolittle. They wont ask you twice.

DOOLITTLE. It aint the lecturing I mind. I'll lecture them blue in the face, I will, and not turn a hair. It's making a gentleman of me that I object to. Who asked him to make a gentleman of me? I was happy. I was free. I touched pretty nigh everybody for money when I wanted it, same as I touched you, Enry Iggins. Now I am worried; tied neck and heels; and everybody touches me for money. It's a fine thing for you, says my solicitor. Is it? says I. You mean it's a good thing for you, I says. When I was a poor man and had a solicitor once when they found a pram in the dust cart, he got me off, and got shut of me and got me shut of him as quick as he could. Same with the doctors: used to shove me out of the hospital before I could hardly stand on my legs, and nothing to pay. Now they finds out that I'm not a healthy man and cant live unless they looks after me twice a day. In the house I'm not let do a hand's turn for myself: somebody else must do it and touch me for it. A year ago I hadnt a relative in the world except two or three that wouldnt speak to me. Now Ive fifty, and not a decent week's wages among the lot of them. I have to live for others and not for myself: that middle class morality. You talk of losing Eliza. Dont you be anxious: I bet she's on my doorstep by this: she that could support herself easy by selling flowers if I wasnt respectable. And the next one to touch me will be you, Enry Iggins. I'll have to learn to speak middle class language from you, instead of speaking proper English. Thats where youll come in; and I daresay thats what you done it for.

MRS HIGGINS. But, my dear Mr Doolittle, you need not suffer all this if you are really in earnest. Nobody can force you to accept this bequest. You can repudiate it. Isnt that so, Colonel Pickering?

PICKERING. I believe so.

DOOLITTLE [softening his manner in deference to her sex] Thats the tragedy of it, maam. It's easy to say chuck it; but I havnt the nerve. Which of us has? We're all intimidated. Intimidated, maam: thats what we are. What is there for me if I chuck it but the workhouse in my old age? I have to dye my hair already to keep my job as a dustman. If I was one of the deserving poor, and had put by a bit, I could chuck it; but then why should I, acause the deserving poor might as well be millionaries for all the happiness they ever has. They dont know what happiness is. But I, as one of the undeserving poor, have nothing between me and the pauper's uniform but this here blasted four thousand a year that shoves me into the middle class. (Excuse the expression, maam; youd use it yourself if you had my provocation.) Theyve got you every way you turn: it's a choice between the Skilly of the workhouse and the Char Bydis of the middle class; and I havnt the nerve for the workhouse. Intimidated: thats what I am. Broke. Bought up. Happier men than me will call for my dust, and touch me for their tip; and I'll look on helpless, and envy them. And thats what your son has brought me to. [*He is overcome by emotion*].

MRS HIGGINS. Well, I'm very glad youre not going to do anything foolish, Mr Doolittle. For this solves the problem of Eliza's future. You can provide for her now.

DOOLITTLE [*with melancholy resignation*] Yes, maam: I'm expected to provide for everyone now, out of four thousand a year.

HIGGINS [*jumping up*] Nonsense! he cant provide for her. He shant provide for her. She doesnt belong to him. I paid him five pounds for her. Doolittle: either youre an honest man or a rogue.

DOOLITTLE [*tolerantly*] A little of both, Henry, like the rest of us: a little of both.

HIGGINS. Well, you took the money for the girl; and you have no right to take her as well.

MRS HIGGINS. Henry: dont be absurd. If you want to know where Eliza is, she is upstairs.

HIGGINS [*amazed*] Upstairs!!! Then I shall jolly soon fetch her downstairs. [*He makes resolutely for the door*].

MRS HIGGINS [*rising and following him*] Be quiet, Henry. Sit down.

HIGGINS. I—

MRS HIGGINS. Sit down, dear; and listen to me.

HIGGINS. Oh very well, very well, very well. [*He throws himself ungraciously on the ottoman, with his face towards the windows*]. But I think you might have told us this half an hour ago.

MRS HIGGINS. Eliza came to me this morning. She told me of the brutal way you two treated her.

HIGGINS [*bounding up again*] What!

PICKERING [*rising also*] My dear Mrs Higgins, she's been telling you stories. We didnt treat her brutally. We hardly said a word to her; and we parted on particularly good terms. [*Turning on Higgins*] Higgins: did you bully her after I went to bed?

HIGGINS. Just the other way about. She threw my slippers in my face. She behaved in the most outrageous way. I never gave her the slightest provocation. The slippers came bang into my face the moment I entered the room—before I had uttered a word. And used perfectly awful language.

PICKERING [*astonished*] But why? What did we do to her?

MRS HIGGINS. I think I know pretty well what you did. The girl is naturally rather affectionate, I think. Isnt she, Mr Doolittle?

DOOLITTLE. Very tender-hearted, maam. Takes after me.

MRS HIGGINS. Just so. She had become attached to you both. She worked very hard for you, Henry. I dont think you quite realize what anything in the nature of brain work means to a girl of her class. Well, it seems that when the great day of trial came, and she did this wonderful thing for you without making a single mistake, you two sat there and never said a word to her, but talked together of how glad you were that it was all over and how you had been bored with the whole thing. And then you were surprised because she threw your slippers at you! *I* should have thrown the fire-irons at you.

HIGGINS. We said nothing except that we were tired and wanted to go to bed. Did we, Pick?

PICKERING [*shrugging his shoulders*] That was all.

MRS HIGGINS [*ironically*] Quite sure?

PICKERING. Absolutely. Really, that was all.

MRS HIGGINS. You didnt thank her, or pet her, or admire her, or tell her how splendid she'd been.

HIGGINS [*impatiently*] But she knew all about that. We didnt make speeches to her, if thats what you mean.

PICKERING [*conscience stricken*] Perhaps we were a little inconsiderate. Is she very angry?

MRS HIGGINS [*returning to her place at the writing-table*] Well, I'm afraid she wont go back to Wimpole Street, especially now that Mr Doolittle is able to keep up the position you have thrust on her; but she says she is quite willing to meet you on friendly terms and to let bygones be bygones.

HIGGINS [*furious*] Is she, by George? Ho!

MRS HIGGINS. If you promise to behave yourself, Henry, I'll ask her to come down. If not, go home; for you have taken up quite enough of my time.

HIGGINS. Oh, all right. Very well. Pick: you behave yourself. Let us put on our best Sunday manners for this creature that we picked out of the mud. [*He flings himself sulkily into the Elizabethan chair*].

DOOLITTLE [*remonstrating*] Now, now, Enry Iggins! Have some consideration for my feelings as a middle class man.

MRS HIGGINS. Remember your promise, Henry. [*She presses the bell-button on the writing-table*]. Mr Doolittle: will you be so good as to step out on the balcony for a moment. I dont want Eliza to have the shock of your news until she has made it up with these two gentlemen. Would you mind?

DOOLITTLE. As you wish, lady. Anything to help Henry to keep her off my hands. [*He disappears through the window*].

The parlormaid answers the bell. Pickering sits down in Doolittle's place.

MRS HIGGINS. Ask Miss Doolittle to come down, please.

THE PARLORMAID. Yes, maam. [*She goes out*].

MRS HIGGINS. Now, Henry: be good.

HIGGINS. I am behaving myself perfectly.

PICKERING. He is doing his best, Mrs Higgins.

A pause. Higgins throws back his head; stretches out his legs; and begins to whistle.

MRS HIGGINS. Henry, dearest, you dont look at all nice in that attitude.

HIGGINS [*pulling himself together*] I was not trying to look nice, mother.

MRS HIGGINS. It doesnt matter, dear. I only wanted to make you speak.

HIGGINS. Why?

MRS HIGGINS. Because you cant speak and whistle at the same time.

Higgins groans. Another very trying pause.

HIGGINS [*springing up, out of patience*] Where the devil is that girl? Are we to wait here all day?

Eliza enters, sunny, self-possessed, and giving a staggeringly convincing exhibition of ease of manner. She carries a little workbasket, and is very much at home. Pickering is too much taken aback to rise.

LIZA. How do you do, Professor Higgins? Are you quite well?

HIGGINS [*choking*] Am I—[*He can say no more*].

LIZA. But of course you are: you are never ill. So glad to see you again, Colonel Pickering. [*He rises hastily; and they shake hands*]. Quite chilly this morning, isnt it? [*She sits down on his left. He sits beside her*].

HIGGINS. Dont you dare try this game on me. I taught it to

you; and it doesnt take me in. Get up and come home; and dont be a fool.

Eliza takes a piece of needlework from her basket, and begins to stitch at it, without taking the least notice of this outburst.

MRS HIGGINS. Very nicely put, indeed, Henry. No woman could resist such an invitation.

HIGGINS. You let her alone, mother. Let her speak for herself. You will jolly soon see whether she has an idea that I havnt put into her head or a word that I havnt put into her mouth. I tell you I have created this thing out of the squashed cabbage leaves of Covent Garden; and now she pretends to play the fine lady with me.

MRS HIGGINS [*placidly*] Yes, dear; but youll sit down, wont you?

Higgins sits down again, savagely.

LIZA [*to Pickering, taking no apparent notice of Higgins, and working away deftly*] Will you drop me altogether now that the experiment is over, Colonel Pickering?

PICKERING. Oh dont. You mustnt think of it as an experiment. It shocks me, somehow.

LIZA. Oh, I'm only a squashed cabbage leaf—

PICKERING [*impulsively*] No.

LIZA [*continuing quietly*] —but I owe so much to you that I should be very unhappy if you forgot me.

PICKERING. It's very kind of you to say so, Miss Doolittle.

LIZA. It's not because you paid for my dresses. I know you are generous to everybody with money. But it was from you that I learnt really nice manners; and that is what makes one a lady, isnt it? You see it was so very difficult for me with the example of Professor Higgins always before me. I was brought up to be just like him, unable to control myself, and using bad language on the slightest provocation. And I should never have known that ladies and gentlemen didnt behave like that if you hadnt been there.

HIGGINS. Well!!

PICKERING. Oh, thats only his way, you know. He doesnt mean it.

LIZA. Oh, *I* didnt mean it either, when I was a flower girl. It was only my way. But you see I did it; and thats what makes the difference after all.

PICKERING. No doubt. Still, he taught you to speak; and I couldnt have done that, you know.

LIZA [*trivially*] Of course: that is his profession.

HIGGINS. Damnation!

LIZA [*continuing*] It was just like learning to dance in the fashionable way: there was nothing more than that in it. But do you know what began my real education?

PICKERING. What?

LIZA [*stopping her work for a moment*] Your calling me Miss Doolittle that day when I first came to Wimpole Street. That was the beginning of self-respect for me. [*She resumes her stitching*]. And there were a hundred little things you never noticed, because they came naturally to you. Things about standing up and taking off your hat and opening doors—

PICKERING. Oh, that was nothing.

LIZA. Yes: things that shewed you thought and felt about me as if I were something better than a scullery-maid; though of course I know you would have been just the same to a scullery-maid if she had been let into the drawing room. You never took off your boots in the dining room when I was there.

PICKERING. You mustnt mind that. Higgins takes off his boots all over the place.

LIZA. I know. I am not blaming him. It is his way, isnt it? But it made such a difference to me that you didnt do it. You see, really and truly, apart from the things anyone can pick up (the dressing and the proper way of speaking, and so on), the difference between a lady and a flower girl is not how she behaves, but how she's treated. I shall always be a flower girl to Professor Higgins, because he always treats me as a flower girl, and always will; but I know I can be a lady to you, because you always treat me as a lady, and always will.

MRS HIGGINS. Please dont grind your teeth, Henry.

PICKERING. Well, this is really very nice of you, Miss Doolittle.

LIZA. I should like you to call me Eliza, now, if you would.

PICKERING. Thank you, Eliza, of course.

LIZA. And I should like Professor Higgins to call me Miss Doolittle.

HIGGINS. I'll see you damned first.

MRS HIGGINS. Henry! Henry!

PICKERING [*laughing*] Why dont you slang back at him? Dont stand it. It would do him a lot of good.

LIZA. I cant. I could have done it once; but now I cant go back to it. You told me, you know, that when a child is brought to a foreign country, it picks up the language in a few weeks, and forgets its own. Well, I am a child in your country. I have forgotten my own language, and can speak nothing but yours. Thats the real break-off with the corner of Tottenham Court Road. Leaving Wimpole Street finishes it.

PICKERING [*much alarmed*] Oh! but youre coming back to Wimpole Street, arnt you? Youll forgive Higgins?

HIGGINS [*rising*] Forgive! Will she, by George! Let her go. Let her find out how she can get on without us. She will relapse into the gutter in three weeks without me at her elbow.

Doolittle appears at the centre window. With a look of dignified reproach at Higgins, he comes slowly and silently to his daughter, who, with her back to the window, is unconscious of his approach.

PICKERING. He's incorrigible, Eliza. You wont relapse, will you?

LIZA. No: not now. Never again. I have learnt my lesson. I dont believe I could utter one of the old sounds if I tried. [*Doolittle touches her on the left shoulder. She drops her work, losing her self-possession utterly at the spectacle of her father's splendor*] A-a-a-a-ah-ow-ooh!

HIGGINS [*with a crow of triumph*] Aha! Just so. A-a-a-a-ahowooh! A-a-a-a-ahowooh! A-a-a-a-ahowooh! Victory! Victory! [*He throws himself on the divan, folding his arms, and spraddling arrogantly*].

DOOLITTLE. Can you blame the girl? Dont look at me like that, Eliza. It aint my fault. Ive come into some money.

LIZA. You must have touched a millionaire this time, dad.

DOOLITTLE. I have. But I'm dressed something special today. I'm going to St George's, Hanover Square. Your stepmother is going to marry me.

LIZA [*angrily*] Youre going to let yourself down to marry that low common woman!

PICKERING [*quietly*] He ought to, Eliza. [*To Doolittle*] Why has she changed her mind?

DOOLITTLE [*sadly*] Intimidated, Governor. Intimidated. Middle class morality claims its victim. Wont you put on your hat, Liza, and come and see me turned off?

LIZA. If the Colonel says I must, I—I'll [*almost sobbing*] I'll demean myself. And get insulted for my pains, like enough.

DOOLITTLE. Dont be afraid: she never comes to words with anyone now, poor woman! respectability has broke all the spirit out of her.

PICKERING [*squeezing Eliza's elbow gently*] Be kind to them, Eliza. Make the best of it.

LIZA [*forcing a little smile for him through her vexation*] Oh well, just to shew theres no ill feeling. I'll be back in a moment. [*She goes out*].

DOOLITTLE [*sitting down beside Pickering*] I feel uncommon nervous about the ceremony, Colonel. I wish youd come and see me through it.

PICKERING. But youve been through it before, man. You were married to Eliza's mother.

DOOLITTLE. Who told you that, Colonel?

PICKERING. Well, nobody told me. But I concluded—naturally—

DOOLITTLE. No: that aint the natural way, Colonel: it's only the middle class way. My way was always the undeserving way. But dont say nothing to Eliza. She dont know: I always had a delicacy about telling her.

PICKERING. Quite right. We'll leave it so, if you dont mind.

DOOLITTLE. And youll come to the church, Colonel, and put me through straight?

PICKERING. With pleasure. As far as a bachelor can.

MRS HIGGINS. May I come, Mr Doolittle? I should be very sorry to miss your wedding.

DOOLITTLE. I should indeed be honored by your condescension, maam; and my poor old woman would take it as a tremenjous compliment. She's been very low, thinking of the happy days that are no more.

MRS HIGGINS [*rising*] I'll order the carriage and get ready. [*The men rise, except Higgins*]. I shant be more than fifteen minutes. [*As she goes to the door Eliza comes in, hatted and buttoning her gloves*]. I'm going to the church to see your father married, Eliza. You had better come in the brougham with me. Colonel Pickering can go on with the bridegroom.

Mrs Higgins goes out. Eliza comes to the middle of the room between the centre window and the ottoman. Pickering joins her.

DOOLITTLE. Bridegroom. What a word! It makes a man realize his position, somehow. [*He takes up his hat and goes towards the door*].

PICKERING. Before I go, Eliza, do forgive Higgins and come back to us.

LIZA. I dont think dad would allow me. Would you, dad?

DOOLITTLE [*sad but magnanimous*] They played you off very cunning, Eliza, them two sportsmen. If it had been only one of them, you could have nailed him. But you see, there was two; and one of them chaperoned the other, as you might say. [*To Pickering*] It was artful of you, Colonel; but I bear no malice: I should have done the same myself. I been the victim of one woman after another all my life, and I dont grudge you two getting the better of Liza. I shant interfere. It's time for us to go. Colonel. So long, Henry. See you in St George's, Eliza. [*He goes out*].

PICKERING [*coaxing*] Do stay with us, Eliza. [*He follows Doolittle*].

Eliza goes out on the balcony to avoid being alone with Higgins. He rises and joins her there. She immediately comes back into the room and makes for the door; but he goes along the balcony and gets his back to the door before she reaches it.

HIGGINS. Well Eliza, youve had a bit of your own back, as you call it. Have you had enough? and are you going to be reasonable? Or do you want any more?

LIZA. You want me back only to pick up your slippers and put up with your tempers and fetch and carry for you.

HIGGINS. I havnt said I wanted you back at all.

LIZA. Oh, indeed. Then what are we talking about?

HIGGINS. About you, not about me. If you come back I shall treat you just as I have always treated you. I cant change my nature; and dont intend to change my manners. My manners are exactly the same as Colonel Pickering's.

LIZA. Thats not true. He treats a flower girl as if she was a duchess.

HIGGINS. And I treat a duchess as if she was a flower girl.

LIZA. I see [*She turns away composedly, and sits on the ottoman, facing the window*]. The same to everybody.

HIGGINS. Just so.

LIZA. Like father.

HIGGINS [*grinning, a little taken down*] Without accepting the comparison at all points, Eliza, it's quite true that your father is not a snob, and that he will be quite at home in any station of life to which his eccentric destiny may call him. [*Seriously*] The great secret, Eliza, is not having bad manners or good manners or any other particular sort of manners, but having the same manner for all human souls: in short, behaving as if you were in Heaven, where there are no third-class carriages, and one soul is as good as another.

LIZA. Amen. You are a born preacher.

HIGGINS [*irritated*] The question is not whether I treat you rudely, but whether you ever heard me treat anyone else better.

LIZA [*with sudden sincerity*] I dont care how you treat me. I dont mind your swearing at me. I shouldnt mind a black eye: Ive had one before this. But [*standing up and facing him*] I wont be passed over.

HIGGINS. Then get out of my way; for I wont stop for you. You talk about me as if I were a motor bus.

LIZA. So you are a motor bus: all bounce and go, and no consideration for anyone. But I can do without you: dont think I cant.

HIGGINS. I know you can. I told you you could.

LIZA [*wounded, getting away from him to the other side of the ottoman with her face to the hearth*] I know you did, you brute. You wanted to get rid of me.

HIGGINS. Liar.

LIZA. Thank you. [*She sits down with dignity*].

HIGGINS. You never asked yourself, I suppose, whether *I* could do without you.

LIZA [*earnestly*] Dont you try to get round me. Youll have to do without me.

HIGGINS [*arrogant*] I can do without anybody. I have my own soul: my own spark of divine fire. But [*with sudden humility*] I shall miss you, Eliza. [*He sits down near her on the ottoman*] I have learnt something from your idiotic notions: I confess that humbly and gratefully. And I have grown accustomed to your voice and appearance. I like them, rather.

LIZA. Well, you have both of them on your gramophone

and in your book of photographs. When you feel lonely without me, you can turn the machine on. It's got no feelings to hurt.

HIGGINS. I cant turn your soul on. Leave me those feelings; and you can take away the voice and the face. They are not you.

LIZA. Oh, you are a devil. You can twist the heart in a girl as easy as some could twist her arms to hurt her. Mrs Pearce warned me. Time and again she has wanted to leave you; and you always got round her at the last minute. And you dont care a bit for her. And you dont care a bit for me.

HIGGINS. I care for life, for humanity; and you are a part of it that has come my way and been built into my house. What more can you or anyone ask?

LIZA. I wont care for anybody that doesnt care for me.

HIGGINS. Commercial principles, Eliza. Like [*reproducing her Covent Garden pronunciation with professional exactness*] s'yollin voylets [*selling violets*], isnt it?

LIZA. Dont sneer at me. It's mean to sneer at me.

HIGGINS. I have never sneered in my life. Sneering doesnt become either the human face or the human soul. I am expressing my righteous contempt for Commercialism. I dont and wont trade in affection. You call me a brute because you couldnt buy a claim on me by fetching my slippers and finding my spectacles. You were a fool: I think a woman fetching a man's slippers is a disgusting sight: did I ever fetch your slippers? I think a good deal more of you for throwing them in my face. No use slaving for me and then saying you want to be cared for: who cares for a slave? If you come back, come back for the sake of good fellowship; for youll get nothing else. Youve had a thousand times as much out of me as I have out of you; and if you dare to set up your little dog's tricks of fetching and carrying slippers against my creation of a Duchess Eliza, I'll slam the door in your silly face.

LIZA. What did you do it for if you didnt care for me?

HIGGINS [*heartily*] Why, because it was my job.

LIZA. You never thought of the trouble it would make for me.

HIGGINS. Would the world ever have been made if its maker had been afraid of making trouble? Making life means making trouble. Theres only one way of escaping trouble;

and thats killing things. Cowards, you notice, are always shrieking to have troublesome people killed.

LIZA. I'm no preacher: I dont notice things like that. I notice that you dont notice me.

HIGGINS [*jumping up and walking about intolerantly*] Eliza: youre an idiot. I waste the treasures of my Miltonic mind by spreading them before you. Once for all, understand that I go my way and do my work without caring twopence what happens to either of us. I am not intimidated, like your father and your stepmother. So you can come back or go to the devil: which you please.

LIZA. What am I to come back for?

HIGGINS [*bouncing up on his knees on the ottoman and leaning over it to her*] For the fun of it. Thats why I took you on.

LIZA [*with averted face*] And you may throw me out to-morrow if I dont do everything you want me to?

HIGGINS. Yes; and you may walk out tomorrow if I dont do everything you want me to.

LIZA. And live with my stepmother?

HIGGINS. Yes, or sell flowers.

LIZA. Oh! if I only could go back to my flower basket! I should be independent of both you and father and all the world! Why did you take my independence from me? Why did I give it up? I'm a slave now, for all my fine clothes.

HIGGINS. Not a bit. I'll adopt you as my daughter and settle money on you if you like. Or would you rather marry Pickering?

LIZA [*looking fiercely round at him*] I wouldnt marry you if you asked me; and youre nearer my age than what he is.

HIGGINS [*gently*] Than he is: not "than what he is."

LIZA [*losing her temper and rising*] I'll talk as I like. Youre not my teacher now.

HIGGINS [*reflectively*] I dont suppose Pickering would, though. He's as confirmed an old bachelor as I am.

LIZA. Thats not what I want; and dont you think it. Ive always had chaps enough wanting me that way. Freddy Hill writes to me twice and three times a day, sheets and sheets.

HIGGINS [*disagreeably surprised*] Damn his impudence! [*He recoils and finds himself sitting on his heels*].

LIZA. He has a right to if he likes, poor lad. And he does love me.

HIGGINS [*getting off the ottoman*] You have no right to encourage him.

LIZA. Every girl has a right to be loved.

HIGGINS. What! By fools like that?

LIZA. Freddy's not a fool. And if he's weak and poor and
wants me, may be he'd make me happier than my betters
that bully me and dont want me.

HIGGINS. Can he make anything of you? Thats the point.

LIZA. Perhaps I could make something of him. But I never
thought of us making anything of one another; and you never
think of anything else. I only want to be natural.

HIGGINS. In short, you want me to be as infatuated about
you as Freddy? Is that it?

LIZA. No I dont. Thats not the sort of feeling I want from
you. And dont you be too sure of yourself or of me. I could
have been a bad girl if I'd liked. Ive seen more of some things
than you, for all your learning. Girls like me can drag gentlemen down to make love to them easy enough. And they
wish each other dead the next minute.

HIGGINS. Of course they do. Then what in thunder are we
quarrelling about?

LIZA [*much troubled*] I want a little kindness. I know I'm
a common ignorant girl, and you a book-learned gentleman;
but I'm not dirt under your feet. What I done [*correcting
herself*] what I did was not for the dresses and the taxis: I
did it because we were pleasant together and I come—came—
to care for you; not to want you to make love to me, and not
forgetting the difference between us, but more friendly like.

HIGGINS. Well, of course. Thats just how I feel. And how
Pickering feels. Eliza: youre a fool.

LIZA. Thats not a proper answer to give me [*she sinks on
the chair at the writing-table in tears*].

HIGGINS. It's all youll get until you stop being a common
idiot. If youre going to be a lady, youll have to give up feeling neglected if the men you know dont spend half their
time snivelling over you and the other half giving you black
eyes. If you cant stand the coldness of my sort of life, and
the strain of it, go back to the gutter. Work til youre more a
brute than a human being; and then cuddle and squabble
and drink til you fall asleep. Oh, it's a fine life, the life of the
gutter. It's real: it's warm: it's violent: you can feel it through
the thickest skin: you can taste it and smell it without any

training or any work. Not like Science and Literature and
Classical Music and Philosophy and Art. You find me cold,
unfeeling, selfish, dont you? Very well: be off with you to
the sort of people you like. Marry some sentimental hog or
other with lots of money, and a thick pair of lips to kiss
you with and a thick pair of boots to kick you with. If you
cant appreciate what youve got, youd better get what you
can appreciate.

LIZA [*desperate*] Oh, you are a cruel tyrant. I cant talk to
you: you turn everything against me: I'm always in the
wrong. But you know very well all the time that youre
nothing but a bully. You know I cant go back to the gutter,
as you call it, and that I have no real friends in the world but
you and the Colonel. You know well I couldnt bear to live
with a low common man after you two; and it's wicked and
cruel of you to insult me by pretending I could. You think
I must go back to Wimpole Street because I have nowhere
else to go but father's. But dont you be too sure that you
have me under your feet to be trampled on and talked down.
I'll marry Freddy, I will, as soon as I'm able to support him.

HIGGINS [*thunderstruck*] Freddy!!! that young fool! That
poor devil who couldn't get a job as an errand boy even if he
had the guts to try for it! Woman: do you not understand
that I have made you a consort for a king?

LIZA. Freddy loves me: that makes him king enough for
me. I dont want him to work: he wasnt brought up to it as
I was. I'll go and be a teacher.

HIGGINS. Whatll you teach, in heaven's name?

LIZA. What you taught me. I'll teach phonetics.

HIGGINS. Ha! ha! ha!

LIZA. I'll offer myself as an assistant to that hairyfaced
Hungarian.

HIGGINS [*rising in a fury*] What! That imposter! that hum-
bug! that toadying ignoramus! Teach him my methods! my
discoveries! You take one step in his direction and I'll wring
your neck. [*He lays hands on her*]. Do you hear?

LIZA [*defiantly non-resistant*] Wring away. What do I care?
I knew youd strike me some day. [*He lets her go, stamping
with rage at having forgotten himself, and recoils so hastily
that he stumbles back into his seat on the ottoman*]. Aha!
Now I know how to deal with you. What a fool I was not to
think of it before! You cant take away the knowledge you

gave me. You said I had a finer ear than you. And I can be civil and kind to people, which is more than you can. Aha! [*Purposely dropping her aitches to annoy him*] Thats done you, Enry Iggins, it az. Now I dont care that [*snapping her fingers*] for your bullying and your big talk. I'll advertize it in the papers that your duchess is only a flower girl that you taught, and that she'll teach anybody to be a duchess just the same in six months for a thousand guineas. Oh, when I think of myself crawling under your feet and being trampled on and called names, when all the time I had only to lift up my finger to be as good as you, I could just kick myself.

HIGGINS [*wondering at her*] You damned impudent slut, you! But it's better than snivelling; better than fetching slippers and finding spectacles, isnt it? [*Rising*] By George, Eliza, I said I'd make a woman of you; and I have. I like you like this.

LIZA. Yes: you turn round and make up to me now that I'm not afraid of you, and can do without you.

HIGGINS. Of course I do, you little fool. Five minutes ago you were like a millstone round my neck. Now youre a tower of strength: a consort battleship. You and I and Pickering will be three old bachelors instead of only two men and a silly girl.

Mrs Higgins returns, dressed for the wedding. Eliza instantly becomes cool and elegant.

MRS HIGGINS. The carriage is waiting, Eliza. Are you ready?

LIZA. Quite. Is the Professor coming?

MRS HIGGINS. Certainly not. He cant behave himself in church. He makes remarks out loud all the time on the clergyman's pronunciation.

LIZA. Then I shall not see you again, Professor. Goodbye. [*She goes to the door*].

MRS HIGGINS [*coming to Higgins*] Goodbye, dear.

HIGGINS. Goodbye, mother. [*He is about to kiss her, when he recollects something*]. Oh, by the way, Eliza, order a ham and a Stilton cheese, will you? And buy me a pair of reindeer gloves, number eights, and a tie to match that new suit of mine. You can choose the color. [*His cheerful, careless, vigorous voice shews that he is incorrigible*].

LIZA [*disdainfully*] Number eights are too small for you if you want them lined with lamb's wool. You have three new ties that you have forgotten in the drawer of your washstand. Colonel Pickering prefers double Gloucester to Stilton;

and you dont notice the difference. I telephoned Mrs Pearce this morning not to forget the ham. What you are to do without me I cannot imagine. [*She sweeps out*].

MRS HIGGINS. I'm afraid youve spoilt that girl, Henry. I should be uneasy about you and her if she were less fond of Colonel Pickering.

HIGGINS. Pickering! Nonsense: she's going to marry Freddy. Ha ha! Freddy! Freddy! ! Ha ha ha ha ha! ! ! ! ! [*He roars with laughter as the play ends*].

The rest of the story need not be shewn in action, and indeed, would hardly need telling if our imaginations were not so enfeebled by their lazy dependence on the ready-mades and reach-me-downs of the ragshop in which Romance keeps its stock of "happy endings" to misfit all stories. Now, the history of Eliza Doolittle, though called a romance because the transfiguration it records seems exceedingly improbable, is common enough. Such transfigurations have been achieved by hundreds of resolutely ambitious young women since Nell Gwynne set them the example by playing queens and fascinating kings in the theatre in which she began by selling oranges. Nevertheless, people in all directions have assumed, for no other reason than that she became the heroine of a romance, that she must have married the hero of it. This is unbearable, not only because her little drama, if acted on such a thoughtless assumption, must be spoiled, but because the true sequel is patent to anyone with a sense of human nature in general, and of feminine instinct in particular.

Eliza, in telling Higgins she would not marry him if he asked her, was not coquetting: she was announcing a well-considered decision. When a bachelor interests, and dominates, and teaches, and becomes important to a spinster, as Higgins with Eliza, she always, if she has character enough to be capable of it, considers very seriously indeed whether she will play for becoming that bachelor's wife, especially if he is so little interested in marriage that a determined and devoted woman might capture him if she set herself resolutely to do it. Her decision will depend a good deal on whether she is really free to choose; and that, again, will depend on her age and income. If she is at the end of her youth, and has no security for her livelihood, she will marry him because she must marry anybody who will provide for her. But at Eliza's age a good-looking girl does not feel that pressure: she feels free to pick and choose. She is therefore guided by her instinct in the matter. Eliza's instinct tells her not to marry Higgins. It does not tell her to give him up. It

is not in the slightest doubt as to his remaining one of the
strongest personal interests in her life. It would be very sorely
strained if there was another woman likely to supplant her
with him. But as she feels sure of him on that last point, she
has no doubt at all as to her course, and would not have any,
even if the difference of twenty years in age, which seems
so great to youth, did not exist between them.

As our own instincts are not appealed to by her conclu-
sions, let us see whether we cannot discover some reason in it.
When Higgins excused his indifference to young women on
the ground that they had an irresistible rival in his mother,
he gave the clue to his inveterate old-bachelordom. The case
is uncommon only to the extent that remarkable mothers are
uncommon. If an imaginative boy has a sufficiently rich
mother who has intelligence, personal grace, dignity of character without harshness, and a cultivated sense of the best art
of her time to enable her to make her house beautiful, she
sets a standard for him against which very few women can
struggle, besides effecting for him a disengagement of his
affections, his sense of beauty, and his idealism from his
specifically sexual impulses. This makes him a standing puzzle to the huge number of uncultivated people who have
been brought up in tasteless homes by commonplace or disagreeable parents, and to whom, consequently, literature,
painting, sculpture, music, and affectionate personal relations
come as modes of sex if they come at all. The word passion
means nothing else to them; and that Higgins could have a
passion for phonetics and idealize his mother instead of
Eliza, would seem to them absurd and unnatural. Nevertheless, when we look round and see that hardly anyone is too
ugly or disagreeable to find a wife or a husband if he or she
wants one, whilst many old maids and bachelors are above
the average in quality and culture, we cannot help suspect-
ing that the disentanglement of sex from the associations
with which it is so commonly confused, a disentanglement
which persons of genius achieve by sheer intellectual analysis,
is sometimes produced or aided by parental fascination.

Now, though Eliza was incapable of thus explaining to
herself Higgins's formidable powers of resistance to the
charm that prostrated Freddy at the first glance, she was
instinctively aware that she could never obtain a complete
grip of him, or come between him and his mother (the first

necessity of the married woman). To put it shortly, she knew that for some mysterious reason he had not the makings of a married man in him, according to her conception of a husband as one to whom she would be his nearest and fondest and warmest interest. Even had there been no mother-rival, she would still have refused to accept an interest in herself that was secondary to philosophic interests. Had Mrs Higgins died, there would still have been Milton and the Universal Alphabet. Landor's remark that to those who have the greatest power of loving, love is a secondary affair, would not have recommended Landor to Eliza. Put that along with her resentment of Higgins's domineering superiority, and her mistrust of his coaxing cleverness in getting round her and evading her wrath when he had gone too far with his impetuous bullying, and you will see that Eliza's instinct had good grounds for warning her not to marry her Pygmalion.

And now, whom did Eliza marry? For if Higgins was a predestinate old bachelor, she was most certainly not a predestinate old maid. Well, that can be told very shortly to those who have not guessed it from the indications she has herself given them.

Almost immediately after Eliza is stung into proclaiming her considered determination not to marry Higgins, she mentions the fact that young Mr. Frederick Eynsford Hill is pouring out his love for her daily through the post. Now Freddy is young, practically twenty years younger than Higgins: he is a gentleman (or, as Eliza would qualify him, a toff), and speaks like one. He is nicely dressed, is treated by the Colonel as an equal, loves her unaffectedly, and is not her master, nor ever likely to dominate her in spite of his advantage of social standing. Eliza has no use for the foolish romantic tradition that all women love to be mastered, if not actually bullied and beaten. "When you go to women" says Nietzsche "take your whip with you." Sensible despots have never confined that precaution to women: they have taken their whips with them when they have dealt with men, and been slavishly idealized by the men over whom they have flourished the whip much more than by women. No doubt there are slavish women as well as slavish men; and women, like men, admire those that are stronger than themselves. But to admire a strong person and to live under that strong

person's thumb are two different things. The weak may not
be admired and hero-worshipped; but they are by no means
disliked or shunned; and they never seem to have the least
difficulty in marrying people who are too good for them.
They may fail in emergencies; but life is not one long emergency: it is mostly a string of situations for which no excep-
tional strength is needed, and with which even rather weak
people can cope if they have a stronger partner to help them
out. Accordingly, it is a truth everywhere in evidence that
strong people, masculine or feminine, not only do not marry
stronger people, but do not shew any preference for them
in selecting their friends. When a lion meets another with
a louder roar "the first lion thinks the last a bore." The man
or woman who feels strong enough for two, seeks for every
other quality in a partner than strength.

The converse is also true. Weak people want to marry
strong people who do not frighten them too much; and this
often leads them to make the mistake we describe metaphori-
cally as "biting off more than they can chew." They want
too much for too little; and when the bargain is unreasonable beyond all bearing, the union becomes impossible: it
ends in the weaker party being either discarded or borne as
a cross, which is worse. People who are not only weak, but
silly or obtuse as well, are often in these difficulties.

This being the state of human affairs, what is Eliza fairly
sure to do when she is placed between Freddy and Higgins?
Will she look forward to a lifetime of fetching Higgins's
slippers or to a lifetime of Freddy fetching hers? There can
be no doubt about the answer. Unless Freddy is biologically
repulsive to her, and Higgins biologically attractive to a degree that overwhelms all her other instincts, she will, if she
marries either of them, marry Freddy.

And that is just what Eliza did.

Complications ensued; but they were economic, not romantic. Freddy had no money and no occupation. His mother's
jointure, a last relic of the opulence of Largelady Park, had
enabled her to struggle along in Earlscourt with an air of
gentility, but not to procure any serious secondary education
for her children, much less give the boy a profession. A clerk-
ship at thirty shillings a week was beneath Freddy's dignity,
and extremely distasteful to him besides. His prospects con-
sisted of a hope that if he kept up appearances somebody

would do something for him. The something appeared vaguely to his imagination as a private secretaryship or a sinecure of some sort. To his mother it perhaps appeared as a marriage to some lady of means who could not resist her boy's niceness. Fancy her feelings when he married a flower girl who had become disclassed under extraordinary circumstances which were now notorious!

It is true that Eliza's situation did not seem wholly ineligible. Her father, though formerly a dustman, and now fantastically disclassed, had become extremely popular in the smartest society by a social talent which triumphed over every prejudice and every disadvantage. Rejected by the middle class, which he loathed, he had shot up at once into the highest circles by his wit, his dustmanship (which he carried like a banner), and his Nietzschean transcendence of good and evil. At intimate ducal dinners he sat on the right hand of the Duchess; and in country houses he smoked in the pantry and was made much of by the butler when he was not feeding in the dining room and being consulted by cabinet ministers. But he found it almost as hard to do all this on four thousand a year as Mrs Eynsford Hill to live in Earlscourt on an income so pitiably smaller that I have not the heart to disclose its exact figure. He absolutely refused to add the last straw to his burden by contributing to Eliza's support.

Thus Freddy and Eliza, now Mr and Mrs Eynsford Hill, would have spent a penniless honeymoon but for a wedding present of £500 from the Colonel to Eliza. It lasted a long time because Freddy did not know how to spend money, never having had any to spend, and Eliza, socially trained by a pair of old bachelors, wore her clothes as long as they held together and looked pretty, without the least regard to their being many months out of fashion. Still, £500 will not last two young people for ever; and they both knew, and Eliza felt as well, that they must shift for themselves in the end. She could quarter herself on Wimpole Street because it had come to be her home; but she was quite aware that she ought not to quarter Freddy there, and that it would not be good for his character if she did.

Not that the Wimpole Street bachelors objected. When she consulted them, Higgins declined to be bothered about her housing problem when that solution was so simple. Eliza's desire to have Freddy in the house with her seemed of no more importance than if she had wanted an extra piece of bedroom furniture. Pleas as to Freddy's character, and the moral obligation on him to earn his own living, were lost on Higgins. He denied that Freddy had any character, and declared that if he tried to do any useful work some competent person would have the trouble of undoing it: a procedure involving a net loss to the community, and great unhappiness to Freddy himself, who was obviously intended by Nature for such light work as amusing Eliza, which, Higgins declared, was a much more useful and honorable occupation than working in the city. When Eliza referred again to her project of teaching phonetics, Higgins abated not a jot of his violent opposition to it. He said she was not within ten years of being qualified to meddle with his pet subject; and as it was evident that the Colonel agreed with him, she felt she could not go against them in this grave matter, and that she had no right, without Higgins's consent, to exploit the knowledge he had given her; for his knowledge seemed to her as much his private property as his watch: Eliza was no communist. Besides, she was superstitiously devoted to them both, more entirely and frankly after her marriage than before it.

It was the Colonel who finally solved the problem, which had cost him much perplexed cogitation. He one day asked Eliza, rather shyly, whether she had quite given up her notion of keeping a flower shop. She replied that she had thought of it, but had put it out of her head, because the Colonel had said, that day at Mrs Higgins's, that it would never do. The Colonel confessed that when he said that, he had not quite recovered from the dazzling impression of the day before. They broke the matter to Higgins that evening. The sole comment vouchsafed by him very nearly led to a serious quarrel with Eliza. It was to the effect that she would have in Freddy an ideal errand boy.

Freddy himself was next sounded on the subject. He said he had been thinking of a shop himself; though it had presented itself to his pennilessness as a small place in which Eliza should sell tobacco at one counter whilst he sold newspapers at the opposite one. But he agreed that it would be extraordinarily jolly to go early every morning with Eliza to Covent Garden and buy flowers on the scene of their first meeting: a sentiment which earned him many kisses from his wife. He added that he had always been afraid to propose anything of the sort, because Clara would make an awful row about a step that must damage her matrimonial chances, and his mother could not be expected to like it after clinging for so many years to that step of the social ladder on which retail trade is impossible.

This difficulty was removed by an event highly unexpected by Freddy's mother. Clara, in the course of her incursions into those artistic circles which were the highest within her reach, discovered that her conversational qualifications were expected to include a grounding in the novels of Mr H. G. Wells. She borrowed them in various directions so energetically that she swallowed them all within two months. The result was a conversion of a kind quite common today. A modern Acts of the Apostles would fill fifty whole Bibles if anyone were capable of writing it.

Poor Clara, who appeared to Higgins and his mother as a disagreeable and ridiculous person, and to her own mother as in some inexplicable way a social failure, had never seen herself in either light; for, though to some extent ridiculed and mimicked in West Kensington like everybody else there, she was accepted as a rational and normal—or shall we say inevitable?—sort of human being. At worst they called her The Pusher; but to them no more than to herself had it ever occurred that she was pushing the air, and pushing it in a wrong direction. Still, she was not happy. She was growing desperate. Her one asset, the fact that her mother was what the Epsom greengrocer called a carriage lady, had no exchange value, apparently. It had prevented her from getting educated, because the only education she could have afforded was education with the Earlscourt greengrocer's daughter. It had led her to seek the society of her mother's class; and that class simply would not have her, because she was much poorer than the greengrocer, and, far from being able to afford a maid, could not afford even a housemaid, and had to scrape along at home with an illiberally treated general servant. Under such circumstances nothing could give her an air of being a genuine product of Largelady Park. And yet its tradition made her regard a marriage with anyone within her reach as an unbearable humiliation. Commercial people and professional people in a small way were odious to her. She ran after painters and novelists; but she did not charm them; and her bold attempts to pick up and practice artistic and literary talk irritated them. She was, in short, an utter failure, an ignorant, incompetent, pretentious, unwelcome, penniless, useless little snob; and though she did not admit these disqualifications (for nobody ever faces unpleasant truths of this kind until the possibility of a way out dawns on them) she felt their effects too keenly to be satisfied with her position.

Clara had a startling eyeopener when, on being suddenly wakened to enthusiasm by a girl of her own age who dazzled her and produced in her a gushing desire to take her for a model, and gain her friendship, she discovered that this exquisite apparition had graduated from the gutter in a few months time. It shook her so violently, that when Mr H. G. Wells lifted her on the point of his puissant pen, and placed her at the angle of view from which the life she was leading and the society to which she clung appeared in its true relation to real human needs and worthy social structure, he effected a conversion and a conviction of sin comparable to the most sensational feats of General Booth or Gypsy Smith. Clara's snobbery went bang. Life suddenly began to move with her. Without knowing how or why, she began to make friends and enemies. Some of the acquaintances to whom she had been a tedious or indifferent or ridiculous affliction, dropped her: others became cordial. To her amazement she found that some "quite nice" people were saturated with Wells, and that this accessibility to ideas was the secret of their niceness. People she had thought deeply religious, and had tried to conciliate on that tack with disastrous results, suddenly took an interest in her, and revealed a hostility to conventional religion which she had never conceived possible except among the most desperate characters. They made her read Galsworthy; and Galsworthy exposed the vanity of Largelady Park and finished her. It exasperated her to think that the dungeon in which she had languished for so many unhappy years had been unlocked all the time, and that the impulses she had so carefully struggled with and stifled for the sake of keeping well with society, were precisely those by which alone she could have come into any sort of sincere human contact. In the radiance of these discoveries, and the tumult of their reaction, she made a fool of herself as freely and conspicuously as when she so rashly adopted Eliza's expletive in Mrs Higgins's drawing room; for the new-born Wellsian had to find her bearings almost as ridiculously as a baby; but nobody hates a baby for its ineptitudes, or thinks the worse of it for trying to eat the matches; and Clara lost no friends by her follies. They laughed at her to her face this time; and she had to defend herself and fight it out as best she could.

When Freddy paid a visit to Earlscourt (which he never did when he could possibly help it) to make the desolating announcement that he and his Eliza were thinking of blackening the Largelady scutcheon by opening a shop, he found the little household already convulsed by a prior announcement from Clara that she also was going to work in an old furniture shop in Dover Street, which had been started by a fellow Wellsian. This appointment Clara owed, after all, to her old social accomplishment of Push. She had made up her mind that, cost what it might, she would see Mr Wells in the flesh; and she had achieved her end at a garden party. She had better luck than so rash an enterprise deserved. Mr Wells came up to her expectations. Age had not withered him, nor could custom stale his infinite variety in half an hour. His pleasant neatness and compactness, his small hands and feet, his teeming ready brain, his unaffected accessibility, and a certain fine apprehensiveness which stamped him as susceptible from his topmost hair to his tipmost toe, proved irresistible. Clara talked of nothing else for weeks and weeks afterwards. And as she happened to talk to the lady of the furniture shop, and that lady also desired above all things to know Mr Wells and sell pretty things to him, she offered Clara a job on the chance of achieving that end through her.

And so it came about that Eliza's luck held, and the expected opposition to the flower shop melted away. The shop is in the arcade of a railway station not very far from the Victoria and Albert Museum; and if you live in that neighbourhood you may go there any day and buy a buttonhole from Eliza.

Now here is a last opportunity for romance. Would you not like to be assured that the shop was an immense success, thanks to Eliza's charms and her early business experience in Covent Garden? Alas! the truth is the truth: the shop did not pay for a long time, simply because Eliza and her Freddy did not know how to keep it. True, Eliza had not to begin at

the very beginning: she knew the names and prices of the
cheaper flowers; and her elation was unbounded when she
found that Freddy, like all youths educated at cheap, pretentious, and thoroughly inefficient schools, knew a little Latin.
It was very little, but enough to make him appear to her a
Porson or Bentley, and to put him at his ease with botanical
nomenclature. Unfortunately he knew nothing else; and Eliza,
though she could count money up to eighteen shillings or so,
and had acquired a certain familiarity with the language of
Milton from her struggles to qualify herself for winning
Higgins's bet, could not write out a bill without utterly dis-
gracing the establishment. Freddy's power of stating in Latin
that Balbus built a wall and that Gaul was divided into three
parts did not carry with it the slightest knowledge of accounts
or business: Colonel Pickering had to explain to him what a
cheque book and a bank account meant. And the pair were
by no means easily teachable. Freddy backed up Eliza in
her obstinate refusal to believe that they could save money
by engaging a bookkeeper with some knowledge of the business. How, they argued, could you possibly save money by
going to extra expense when you already could not make both
ends meet? But the Colonel, after making the ends meet over
and over again, at last gently insisted; and Eliza, humbled
to the dust by having to beg from him so often, and stung by
the uproarious derision of Higgins, to whom the notion of
Freddy succeeding at anything was a joke that never palled,
grasped the fact that business, like phonetics, has to be
learned.

On the piteous spectacle of the pair spending their eve-
nings in shorthand schools and polytechnic classes, learning
bookkeeping and typewriting with incipient junior clerks,
male and female, from the elementary schools, let me not
dwell. There were even classes at the London School of Economics, and a humble personal appeal to the director of that
institution to recommend a course bearing on the flower business. He, being a humorist, explained to them the method of
the celebrated Dickensian essay on Chinese Metaphysics by
the gentleman who read an article on China and an article on
Metaphysics and combined the information. He suggested
that they should combine the London School with Kew Gardens. Eliza, to whom the procedure of the Dickensian gentleman seemed perfectly correct (as in fact it was) and not

in the least funny (which was only her ignorance), took the
advice with entire gravity. But the effort that cost her the
deepest humiliation was a request to Higgins, whose pet
artistic fancy, next to Milton's verse, was caligraphy, and who
himself wrote a most beautiful Italian hand, that he would
teach her to write. He declared that she was congenitally incapable of forming a single letter worthy of the least of Milton's words; but she persisted; and again he suddenly threw
himself into the task of teaching her with a combination of
stormy intensity, concentrated patience, and occasional bursts
of interesting disquisition on the beauty and nobility, the
august mission and destiny, of human handwriting. Eliza
ended by acquiring an extremely uncommercial script which
was a positive extension of her personal beauty, and spending
three times as much on stationery as anyone else because certain qualities and shapes on paper became indispensable to
her. She could not even address an envelope in the usual way
because it made the margins all wrong.

Their commercial schooldays were a period of disgrace and
despair for the young couple. They seemed to be learning
nothing about flower shops. At last they gave it up as hopeless, and shook the dust of the shorthand schools, and the
polytechnics, and the London School of Economics from
their feet for ever. Besides, the business was in some mysterious way beginning to take care of itself. They had somehow forgotten their objections to employing other people.
They came to the conclusion that their own way was the best,
and that they had really a remarkable talent for business. The
Colonel, who had been compelled for some years to keep a
sufficient sum on current account at his bankers to make up
their deficits, found that the provision was unnecessary: the
young people were prospering. It is true that there was not
quite fair play between them and their competitors in trade.
Their week-ends in the country cost them nothing, and saved
them the price of their Sunday dinners; for the motor car was
the Colonel's; and he and Higgins paid the hotel bills. Mr
F. Hill, florist and greengrocer (they soon discovered that
there was money in asparagus; and asparagus led to other
vegetables), had an air which stamped the business as classy;
and in private life he was still Frederick Eynsford Hill, Es-
quire. Not that there was any swank about him: nobody but

Eliza knew that he had been christened Frederick Challoner.
Eliza herself swanked like anything.

That is all. That is how it has turned out. It is astonishing
how much Eliza still manages to meddle in the housekeeping at Wimpole Street in spite of the shop and her own
family. And it is notable that though she never nags her
husband, and frankly loves the Colonel as if she were his
favorite daughter, she has never got out of the habit of nag-
ging Higgins that was established on the fatal night when
she won his bet for him. She snaps his head off on the faintest
provocation, or on none. He no longer dares to tease her by
assuming an abysmal inferiority of Freddy's mind to his own.
He storms and bullies and derides; but she stands up to him so
ruthlessly that the Colonel has to ask her from time to time
to be kinder to Higgins; and it is the only request of his that
brings a mulish expression into her face. Nothing but some
emergency or calamity great enough to break down all likes
and dislikes, and throw them both back on their common
humanity—and may they be spared any such trial!—will ever
alter this. She knows that Higgins does not need her, just as
her father did not need her. The very scrupulousness with
which he told her that day that he had become used to having
her there, and dependent on her for all sorts of little services,
and that he should miss her if she went away (it would never
have occurred to Freddy or the Colonel to say anything of
the sort) deepens her inner certainty that she is "no more to
him than them slippers"; yet she has a sense, too, that his
indifference is deeper than the infatuation of commoner souls.
She is immensely interested in him. She has even secret mis-
chievous moments in which she wishes she could get him
alone, on a desert island, away from all ties and with nobody
else in the world to consider, and just drag him off his pedestal
and see him making love like any common man. We all have
private imaginations of that sort. But when it comes to business, to the life that she really leads as distinguished from
the life of dreams and fancies, she likes Freddy and she likes
the Colonel; and she does not like Higgins and Mr Doolittle.
Galatea never does quite like Pygmalion: his relation to her
is too godlike to be altogether agreeable.